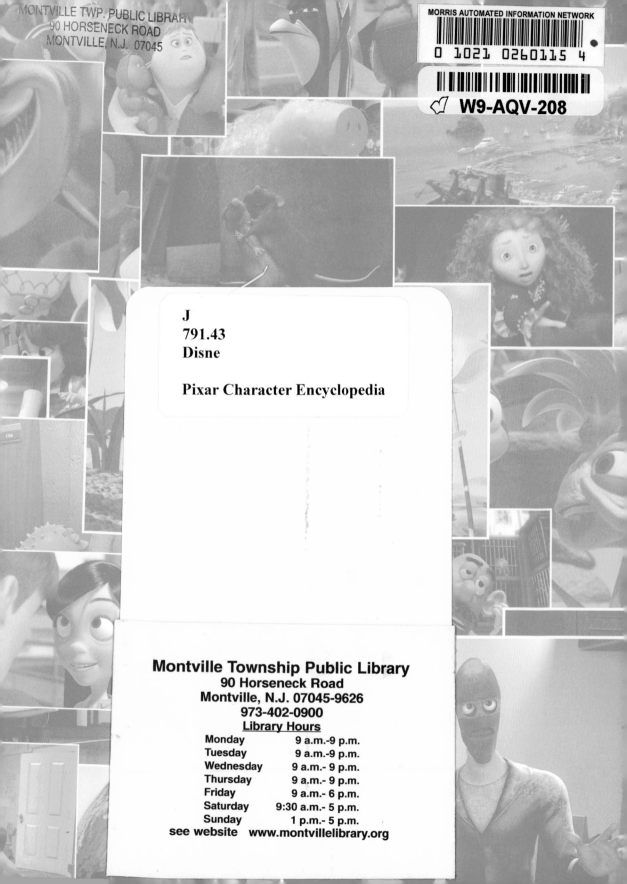

PIXAR
CHARACTER ENCYCLOPEDIA

Written by
**Steve Bynghall,
Jo Casey,
Glenn Dakin,
Clare Hibbert, and
Catherine Saunders**

CONTENTS

This character encyclopedia features more than 200 of Disney•Pixar's best-loved characters, from fearless Finn McMissile to Remy the rodent, from brave Buzz Lightyear to big, bad Bruce the Shark, and many more. The book is organized in chronological order, from *Toy Story* to *Brave*, with any sequels such as *Cars 2* included with the original movie. Look below to find your favorite!

WOODY

HOWDY! SHERIFF WOODY is a rootin', tootin' cowboy doll. He's smart, funny, kind, and the leader of all the toys in Andy's bedroom. The rest of the gang look up to him, and Woody holds regular meetings to keep things running smoothly and safely. He often finds himself in the middle of adventures—not all of them in Andy's imagination!

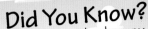

Did You Know?

Woody has had many adventures including car rides, plane escapes, dog chases, and even a close encounter with an incinerator.

Time for a change

With Andy all grown up, the toys panic about what might happen to them. Woody is sure that Andy will look after them, but when the toys are accidentally put out with the trash, no one believes him.

Sheriff's badge

"What matters is we're here for Andy when he needs us."

Rodeo-themed belt buckle

Best buddies

Woody is Andy's favorite toy until Buzz Lightyear shows up. At first, Woody is deeply suspicious of the space ranger, but the two toys eventually become the best of friends and Andy loves them both.

Empty gun holster

Top toy

Woody was once a famous toy, and the star of the black and white TV show *Woody's Roundup*. Nowadays, he is a valuable collector's item, but Woody knows that the most important thing for any toy is to be loved by a kid.

New gang

Sheriff Woody always saves the day! He has the perfect solution to the gang's problem and works out a way to get Andy to donate them to a loving little girl named Bonnie. Now the gang has a new home and a host of new toys to hang out with.

BUZZ LIGHTYEAR

THIS SPACE RANGER comes in peace. He's the coolest toy in the universe and no stranger to embarking on dangerous missions. With his best pal Woody by his side, brave Buzz can take on anything, from nasty neighbors to creepy collectors. The high-tech toy is also a whiz with gadgets and is a natural problem solver.

Protective helmet

Space ranger logo

Facing the truth
When Buzz first arrives, he thinks he's a real space ranger. Woody tries to tell him that he's a toy, but Buzz doesn't believe him— until he sees a Buzz Lightyear commercial. The truth hits Buzz hard.

"This isn't flying, it's falling with style!"

Who's right?
Buzz and Woody can't agree on what's best for the toy gang now Andy is off to college. Woody wants to stay with Andy, but Buzz thinks the toys would be better off at Sunnyside Daycare.

Wrist communicator

Above and beyond
Buzz would go to infinity and beyond for all his pals—he's just that kind of toy. However, two toys hold an extra-special place in the space ranger's heart—his pal Woody and the feisty red-haired cowgirl Jessie.

Did You Know?
If Buzz is switched to Spanish mode, his personality changes dramatically—he becomes romantic, poetic, and loves to dance!

Bendable knee joints

HAMM

ANDY'S PIGGY BANK Hamm is much more than just a cute way of storing loose change. The clever swine is always the first to know what's happening in the outside world. While the other toys rush headlong into adventures, sensible Hamm can usually be seen with his snout in an instruction manual.

Dr. Porkchop
In Andy's games, Hamm plays the evil Dr. Porkchop, but his wicked plans are always foiled by Andy's heroes—Woody and Buzz.

Child's play
Hamm is used to role-playing, but the kids at Sunnyside Daycare are too much for the put–upon pig. Being dunked in glue and covered with glitter and macaroni is just not a good look for him!

"You heard of Kung Fu? Well, get ready for pork chop!"

Slot for loose change

Pig pals
Hamm is good friends with Mr. Potato Head. The cynical pair share a love of wisecracks, playing poker, and expecting the worst in every situation. At Bonnie's house, Hamm finds a new pal in Buttercup. Finally, he has a buddy as brainy as himself!

Pink, plastic body

Trusty trotters

SLINKY

SLINKY DOG IS a toy's best friend and the coiled canine will go to any lengths to help his pals, especially Sheriff Woody. When he's not on dog duty, Slinky likes to relax by playing checkers with Woody. However, sometimes his loyalties can be as flexible as his body.

Divided loyalties
When Buzz arrives, Slinky is impressed by his gadgets. He forgets all about Sheriff Woody for a while.

Streeeeetch
Slinky's body comes in very handy. He is springier than a ladder and stretchier than a rope. He even makes a great fence!

"I knew you were right all along, Woody."

Faithful friend
Slinky is a simple, straightforward kind of hound, so when he sees Woody "injure" Buzz, he turns against his cowboy chum. However, he soon realizes the truth and doesn't hesitate to spring into action and save Woody.

Springy tail

Extendable body

MR. POTATO HEAD

THIS STRAIGHT-TALKING spud is one of the funniest toys in Andy's room. He has a smart mouth (when it's not falling off) and a hard-boiled personality. However, underneath Mr. Potato Head's grumpy exterior is a sensitive guy who just needs the love of a good potato woman.

Versatile veg
Thanks to his detachable body parts, Mr. Potato Head can convey a range of emotions. He also loves to amuse his fellow toys with his clever impressions, such as Potato Picasso.

Ages 3 and up!
Mr. P. H. has always been sensitive about who plays with him. After a toddler play session at Sunnyside Daycare, he feels completely mashed.

Quizzical eyebrows

Stylish hat

"That's Mister Potato Head to you!"

Did You Know?
Mr. Potato Head likes to relax by playing poker with his pal, Hamm. Of course, he is a very bad loser!

Tempestuous tater
In Andy's games, Mr. Potato Head plays the tough bad guy, One-Eyed Bart, but it's not all an act. He has a quick temper and can often jump to the wrong conclusion about his fellow toys.

MRS. POTATO HEAD

THIS ROMANTIC ROOT vegetable is devoted to her husband. In her (detachable) eyes, he is the perfect potato and just needs to be looked after. However, Mrs. Potato Head is no pushover. If Mr. P. H. steps out of line, he can expect a real roasting from the missus.

One potato, two potato
For years, Mr. Potato Head dreamed of a Mrs. Potato Head to share his life with. The devoted pair really are made for each other.

Detachable daisy

"They're so adorable. Let's adopt them!"

Keep an eye out
Having detachable body parts has its advantages. When Mrs. Potato Head leaves one of her eyes in Andy's room, she is able to tell the other toys that Andy didn't really mean to dump them.

Detachable earrings

Earth Mom
Mrs. Potato Head is not only fiercely loyal to her husband, she would also do anything to protect their adopted children. The soft-hearted spud is unofficial Mom to three quirky, squashy Aliens, and, most recently, Bonnie Anderson's cheeky Peas-in-a-Pod.

Did You Know?
Mrs. Potato Head belongs to Andy's sister, Molly, but she lives in Andy's room with her husband.

REX

HE MIGHT LOOK fierce, but Rex is a timid toy who is anxious about everything. He worries that he isn't scary enough, that his roar is too quiet, and that his arms are too short, but Rex's biggest fear is that Andy will find a replacement dinosaur. However, the prehistoric panicker is stronger and braver than he realizes.

Fast fingers
Rex is an obsessive video gamer. His favorite is the Buzz Lightyear game, although he can't press the "fire" and "jump" buttons at the same time due to his small arms.

A sad tail
Rex's long tail is always knocking things over. He just can't control it! Mr. Potato Head gave him the nickname "Godspilla."

"At last! I'm gonna get played with!"

Tiny arms

Dino hero
Rex wishes he was more fierce and fearsome, but the rest of the gang wouldn't have him any other way. After all, he once saved them from the evil Emperor Zurg and helped them to escape from a garbage bag bound for the trash.

Scaly, plastic skin

Big, clumsy feet

BO PEEP

PRETTY PORCELAIN shepherdess Bo Peep is always losing her sheep, but luckily she knows how to hang on to her man. Sheriff Woody is the toy for her and she likes to hook him in with her crook for a special moment. Bo is one of Woody's most loyal supporters and stands by him when the other toys think he has hurt Buzz.

Crook

Porcelain dress

Great acting

Bo Peep usually plays the damsel in distress in Andy's Wild West games, but in reality she is a doll who knows exactly what she wants.

"You're cute when you care."

Did You Know?

Bo is one of many toys who have been lost over years. Rumor has it that she was a yard sale victim. Woody still misses her.

Feeling sheepish

Bo Peep is not a real toy—she is actually the decoration from Molly's lamp. The dainty doll lives by the side of Molly's bed and likes to keep a protective eye out for the toys—and her lost sheep of course.

JESSIE

JESSIE THE yodeling cowgirl puts the "wild" into Wild West. The rough, tough tomboy loves to throw herself into adventures—once she even jumped from a moving plane! Jessie is a fun-loving toy, but she has a deep fear of being abandoned or put into storage.

Hair made of red yarn

Authentic cowgirl belt buckle

Soft side
Woody might be her Sheriff, but there is only one toy for Jessie—Buzz Lightyear. She thinks he is the cutest spaceman she has ever seen. Buzz is equally smitten with the kooky cowgirl, but doesn't know how to show it, unless he is in Spanish mode...

Biggest fear
Jessie used to belong to a little girl named Emily, who loved her very much. However, when Emily grew up she forgot her favorite toy and Jessie was eventually donated to charity.

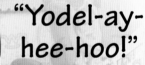

"Yodel-ay-hee-hoo!"

Did You Know?
Jessie was shut away in storage for many years by toy collector Al McWhiggin, until Woody rescued her.

Part of the gang
One of the happiest moments of Jessie's life was when she was reunited with Sheriff Woody and the *Roundup* gang was complete again. Finally getting out of her box and becoming a proper toy again was a dream come true.

Synthetic cow-hide chaps

Cowgirl boots

BULLSEYE

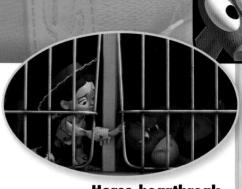

BULLSEYE WAS SHERIFF Woody's trusty steed in *Woody's Roundup*. This happy, hoof-kickin' horse is one of the most trusting and loyal creatures in the toy gang. He can't talk, but his big eyes and expressive body language say it all. Bullseye adores Woody and would do anything for his beloved Sheriff.

Horse heartbreak
When the toys end up at Sunnyside Daycare, Bullseye misses Sheriff Woody terribly.

Big eyes

Did You Know?
Andy printed a letter on the bottom of each of Bullseye's four hooves: A, N, D, and Y. He is a real toy now!

Puppy love
With his big brown eyes, loyal nature, and wagging tail, Bullseye is sometimes more like a giant puppy than a horse. When he is happy, he also loves to lick Woody!

Soft fabric body

Saddle up!
Bullseye specializes in helping Sheriff Woody save the day. However, he also has other talents: He puts his best hoof forward to switch on the video player, dim the lights in Andy's room, and work the TV remote.

Western-style saddle

Imitation leather hooves

LOTSO

LOTSO LOOKS LOVABLE and huggable: He has a soft, plush body, a velvety purple nose, and he smells of strawberries. However, underneath his cuddly exterior, Lotso is a very bitter bear and rules Sunnyside Daycare through fear and intimidation. He causes Andy's toys Lotso trouble!

Toy terror

Andy's toys soon work out who Lotso is really like, but Buzz gets caught spying on him. Lotso tries to make the space toy join his gang, but Buzz refuses. So the gang re-sets Buzz...

Lotso pain

Lotso was once owned by a girl named Daisy, but she left him behind at a picnic. He found his way home, but Daisy had replaced him with another bear. Lotso came to Sunnyside to avoid the heartbreak of being owned, and to take his hurt feelings out on other toys.

Not-so nice

When Andy's toys arrive at Sunnyside, Lotso seems kind and welcoming, but it is all an act. Lotso makes sure that he and his cronies are comfortable, while new toys suffer!

Fake, charming smile

Cuddly body

Walking cane

"You've got a playdate with destiny!"

THE PROSPECTOR

THIS GOLD-DIGGING toy acts like a kindly old-timer, but if you dig a little deeper the Prospector is actually devious and sneaky. The mint-condition meanie has never been taken out of his box and he dreams of being in a museum. He has spent his life on a shelf and he likes it that way!

Detachable hat

Mint-in-the-box

The Prospector is "mint in the box" because he has never been played with or loved by a child. He can't understand why Jessie and Bullseye prefer life outside their packaging. He's a collectable, not a toy!

Did You Know?

In *Woody's Roundup* the spector is nicknamed "Stinky Pete," but in the show he is accident prone, rather than downright mean.

Complete set

When Al McWhiggin buys Woody, the Prospector is delighted and will do anything he can to keep the gang together.

Neckerchief made from the same material as Woody's shirt

Stinky Pete

When Woody decides his place is with Andy and the other toys, the Prospector shows his true colors. He breaks out of his box and does everything he can to stop Woody from leaving.

"No hand-me-down cowboy doll is gonna mess it up for me now."

Plastic pickax

BARBIE

BUBBLY BARBIE CAN'T help being pretty, perky, and permanently upbeat—it's just the way she is made. With her long, blonde, imitation hair, flawless plastic skin, and cute outfits, she always looks fabulous. Even when things get tough, Barbie still dazzles.

Long, blonde hair

Downbeat doll
When Molly's Mom donates Barbie to Sunnyside Daycare, the doll is broken-hearted. Barbie knew that she and Molly were growing apart, but being thrown away is a real shock to her.

Fashionable turquoise unitard

Perfect pair
Things start to look brighter for Barbie at Sunnyside Daycare when she meets Ken. It's love at first sight—they are meant for each other!

Stylish striped leg warmers

"Authority should derive from the consent of the governed, not from threat of force!"

Brainy beauty
Barbie is as smart as she is pretty. She might be in love with Ken, but when she realizes what is truly going on at Sunnyside Daycare, she dumps him. She is loyal to Andy's toys and will not stand by and watch them get hurt.

New start
With Lotso gone, Barbie and the reformed Ken take over Sunnyside. Now Barbie is free to focus on her favorite things—fashion and being kind to other toys.

KEN

DAPPER DOLL KEN is a swinging bachelor with dashing good looks and a perfect plastic physique. He always dresses to impress and even has a room dedicated to trying on clothes in his Dream House. However, Ken's life might be stylish but it is lonely.

Passion for fashion

Barbie is impressed by Ken's extensive wardrobe. He has outfits in every style and for every occasion—from space suits to surf shorts, and tuxedos to tracksuits.

Just his style

Ken knows that he has found his soulmate in Barbie. Not only does she share his love of fashion, she thinks he's smart, too! Not many other toys think that about Ken...

Did You Know?

Ken used to be an astronaut and a hair stylist, but his true calling is co-leader of a new, happy Sunnyside with Barbie.

Safari-style shorts

"No one appreciates clothes here, Barbie! No one."

Hench-doll

Underneath his stylish facade Ken has a dark secret—he works for Lotso. Ken carries out the nightly roll call to ensure no toy has escaped and runs Lotso's creepy casino inside the daycare vending machine.

Cool, blue loafers

Dream House

Ken lives in a deluxe three-story Dream House. It has everything that a cool guy needs, including a disco room, walk-in wardrobe, elevator, and romantic balcony.

17

ALIENS

THE THREE-EYED green Aliens aren't actually from outer space—they're prizes in a game at the *Pizza Planet* restaurant. The squeaky toys all long to be chosen by the all-powerful metal Claw because they think it will lead them to a better place. For three lucky Aliens, that place is Andy's room!

Father figure
These three little Aliens were destined to spend their lives swinging from the rear-view mirror in a *Pizza Planet* truck, until Mr. Potato Head rescued them. Now they call him "Daddy" and would follow him anywhere!

"We are eternally grateful."

Life at Sunnyside
At first, the Aliens think that Sunnyside is great—there are plenty of claw toys. However, when the young kids arrive in the Caterpillar room, the Aliens suffer a serious squishing!

Unlikely heroes
The Aliens' belief in the power of the Claw seems odd to the other toys in Andy's room. However, when the toys are about to be toasted in a trash incinerator, the little green guys know exactly how to save them—with a mechanical claw!

Rubber antenna

Rubber bodies

Pizza Planet logo

WHEEZY

EVER SINCE HIS squeaker broke, Wheezy has been anguishing on Andy's bookshelf feeling sorry for himself. Andy's Mom must have forgotten to get him fixed, and now he's gathered so much dust that he's become asthmatic! The pessimistic penguin is convinced he's destined for the next yard sale.

Reunited
Woody finds Wheezy behind some dusty books. The poor penguin is in low spirits and poor health. Woody tries to cheer him up before he notices that Wheezy is right—Andy's Mom is about to have a yard sale!

'We're all just one stitch away from here..."

Sad expression

Red bow tie

Noble sacrifice
Woody saves Wheezy from the yard sale, but Woody gets sold instead—to toy collector Al McWhiggin.

Flightless wings

Karaoke king
When Wheezy finally gets his squeaker repaired, he is like a brand-new penguin. Penguins might not be able to fly, but this little guy certainly can sing. With a little help from Mike, he puts on a show for the other toys.

ANDY DAVIS

EVERY TOY DESERVES a kid like Andy. Lively and enthusiastic, he has a vivid imagination and loves to play exciting games with his toys. With a few cardboard boxes and some crayons, Andy can create a Wild West town or a space port. Best of all, he treats his toys like pals.

"Now, you gotta promise to take good care of these guys."

Top team
As a little kid, Andy loves all his toys bu Woody and Buzz are his favorites. They are the stars of his games, and the toys whc sleep on his bed at night

Serious expression

Cowboy kid
Every year, Andy goes to Cowboy Camp. He always takes his best pal Woody along for the ride. For Woody, it is a special treat to spend time with Andy, without all the other toys around.

All grown up
The toys watch Andy grow from a sweet little boy into a kind young man. As a grown-up, Andy drives a car, not a make-believe spaceship!

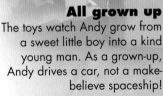

Laptop computer

Growing pains
Now Andy is old enough to go to college, he faces a tough decision about what to do with his toys. Although he hasn't played with them for a while, it is still hard to say goodbye.

MOLLY DAVIS

LIKE MOST LITTLE sisters, Molly has always wanted what her big brother has. First it was his toys, now it is his bedroom. Molly often tried to play with Mr. Potato Head and the rest of the gang, but she wasn't quite as gentle as her brother. When she was a baby, Molly had a tendency to dribble on the toys, so they nicknamed her "Princess Drool!"

Princess Drool
For a while, Andy and Molly shared a room. Molly learned a lot about how to play with toys by watching her big brother, as soon as she was out of her drooling phase...

"Do I still get your room?"

Young lady
Molly likes to think she is as grown up as Andy, but she is still only ten years old. She is more interested in video games, her MP3 player, her cell phone, or reading magazines, rather than playing with toys.

Best brother
Andy and Molly have always been close. Molly will miss her big brother when he goes to college, but at least it means she gets his big bedroom!

Girls' magazine

MP3 player

No dolls!
Molly used to love playing with her Barbie doll, but she is way too grown up for that now. She is happy to donate her Barbie to Sunnyside so another child can play with her.

Fashionable outfit

SID PHILLIPS

ANDY'S NEIGHBOR couldn't be more different than him: While Andy is a caring toy owner, Sid is every toy's worst nightmare! The mixed-up kid doesn't play with his toys, he experiments on them. He enjoys torturing toys and then blowing them up in his yard. No toy ever returns from Sid's house...

Super slob
Sid sleeps on a bare mattress with toy parts, moldy snacks, toy-torturing tools, and dirty clothes littering his filthy bedroom.

Babyhead

Playing with fire
All children know that they shouldn't play with matches, but Sid doesn't care. He loves matches, fireworks, and pretty much anything that is dangerous or horrible!

All better now!
Sid's toys have finally had enough of his experiments. With Sheriff Woody's help, they give him a taste of his own medicine. He doesn't like it!

Scared expression

"Cool! What am I gonna blow up?"

Payback
Like many bullies, underneath it all Sid is a complete coward. When Woody and the other toys break the rules and come to life in front of Sid, the creepy kid runs off screaming!

Skull t-shirt

HANNAH PHILLIPS

IT'S NOT EASY being Sid's little sister. Kind-hearted Hannah not only has to watch out for her big brother's bullying ways, but also her favorite toys keep not-so-mysteriously disappearing to become Sid's experiments. How would you like to find your favorite toy's head attached to the body of a pterodactyl? Poor Hannah...

Poor Janie
Sid thinks that he has made Hannah's Janie doll "all better," but Hannah preferred her without a pterodactyl's head!

Toy tea party
Hannah always takes care of any disturbed toys she finds. After an encounter with Sid, Buzz finds comfort as Mrs. Nesbit in one of Hannah's games.

Did You Know?
Hannah eventually gives Sid some payback. When Sid runs screaming from his toys, Hannah chases him with her doll!

A cool head
Hannah is tougher than she looks. Her toys might be damaged, but she makes the best of a bad situation and hosts tea parties for all her headless dolls.

Cute purple t-shirt

"Mom! Mom, have you seen my Sally doll?"

Broken toy

EMPEROR ZURG

EMPEROR ZURG IS Buzz Lightyear's archenemy. The evil Emperor from the planet Xrghthung has sworn to destroy Buzz and the Galactic Alliance. Freed from his box at *Al's Toy Barn*, Zurg attempts to take over the universe. Like Buzz, he has issues with being a "toy."

> "So, we meet again Buzz Lightyear, for the last time!"

Evil red eyes

Dino defeat
Zurg is defeated by a surprising opponent—Rex. The timid tyrannosaurus thinks that Zurg is winning and can't bear to watch. As he turns away, Rex's clumsy tail sweeps Zurg off his feet. Game over!

Bad Dad
As Zurg and New Buzz do battle, the evil emperor hits the space ranger with an unexpected blow: Zurg reveals he is actually Buzz's father! Against the odds, father and son start to bond.

Evil cape

Almost invincible purple armor

NEW BUZZ

AT *AL'S TOY BARN*, Buzz Lightyear sees a whole aisle of new Buzz action figures. Thankfully, Buzz has come to terms with the fact that he's a toy and is impressed, not confused! However, Buzz is tempted by the new version's utility belt and tries to grab one.

Protective helmet

New model
Buzz can't resist the new utility belt, which has cool anti-gravity buttons and special climbing magnets!

Concealed space wings

Buzz #2
When New Buzz spots someone trying to steal his utility belt, he arrests him immediately! Trapping Buzz in his box, New Buzz sets off on an adventure with the rest of Andy's toys.

Super high-tech utility belt

Who's who?
The other toys think that Buzz is acting weird—he keeps talking about laser beams and booster pods. However, when the real Buzz shows up, they can't tell them apart—until they look under Buzz's space boot and find Andy's name.

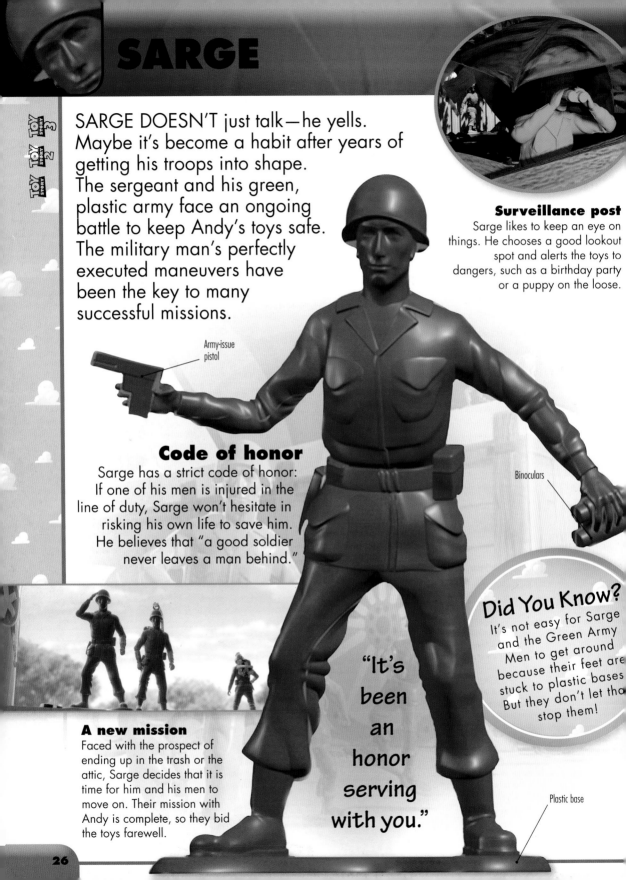

SARGE

SARGE DOESN'T just talk—he yells. Maybe it's become a habit after years of getting his troops into shape. The sergeant and his green, plastic army face an ongoing battle to keep Andy's toys safe. The military man's perfectly executed maneuvers have been the key to many successful missions.

Surveillance post
Sarge likes to keep an eye on things. He chooses a good lookout spot and alerts the toys to dangers, such as a birthday party or a puppy on the loose.

Army-issue pistol

Code of honor
Sarge has a strict code of honor: If one of his men is injured in the line of duty, Sarge won't hesitate in risking his own life to save him. He believes that "a good soldier never leaves a man behind."

Binoculars

Did You Know?
It's not easy for Sarge and the Green Army Men to get around because their feet are stuck to plastic bases. But they don't let that stop them!

A new mission
Faced with the prospect of ending up in the trash or the attic, Sarge decides that it is time for him and his men to move on. Their mission with Andy is complete, so they bid the toys farewell.

"It's been an honor serving with you."

Plastic base

BUCKET O' SOLDIERS

THE GREEN ARMY Men may be the smallest toys in the toy box, but these highly trained plastic soldiers are ready to face any challenge with teamwork, determination, and good, old-fashioned courage. When humans are around, they are under orders to freeze immediately—even if it means being trodden on by Andy's Mom!

Roger that!
Communication is important for any good army. The Green Army Men commandeer Molly's baby monitor to use as a radio on their top secret missions.

Sarge in charge
The obedient soldiers obey Sarge's orders without hesitation. At his command, the army men will leap from their bucket, parachute down stairs, move heavy equipment, or form an all-out attack.

Machine gun

"Frag him!"
The loyal troops don't question the order to swarm Woody when Sarge thinks he has deliberately pushed Buzz out of the window.

Bomb!

Bazooka

ROBOT

ROBOT ROLLS AROUND to wherever the action is, but he prefers to stay on the sidelines, simply watching. Robot doesn't speak—he flashes his eye lights or raises his arms up and down to communicate with the other toys. Some might say that Robot is the strong, silent type.

One of the gang
As Robot is a pre-school learning toy, he is a simple guy. He likes to follow the crowd and if the rest of the toys think Woody is bad, Robot isn't going to disagree!

Best friends
Robot's best pal is a shy snake toy. When Snake isn't hiding under the bed, he likes to stick close to Robot. Snake and Robot share a common admiration for Buzz, and the friends are happy to help the space ranger mend his cardboard spaceship.

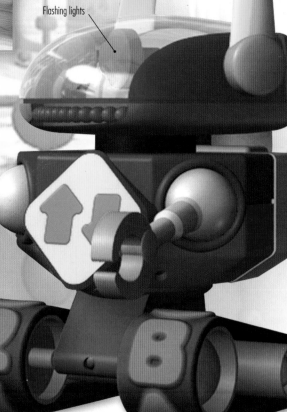

Flashing lights

Pincers for gripping

Treads

Space pals
Robot would bend over backwards to help out his space ranger pal Buzz. Literally. He stands on his head so Buzz can use his feet as a treadmill. Robot doubles as a learning toy and fitness equipment!

RC

THIS REMOTE CONTROLLED car is the fastest toy in Andy's room. In fact, RC has two speeds—fast and turbo! Any chance he gets, RC can be seen speeding, swerving, and skidding around Andy's room—the word "slow" just isn't in his vocabulary. RC has even been known to go off road!

Rev it up!

Like Robot, RC can't talk but he conveys his emotions by revving his engine. It means he is either excited, or scared. That's how he tells the other toys that Woody has "pushed" Buzz out of the window.

Remote control antenna

Teamwork

RC's speed and Slinky's stretching abilities nearly succeed in reuniting the toys, but RC's batteries give out at the crucial moment.

Turbo hero

RC makes up for being wrong about Woody. He tries to give him and Buzz a ride so they can catch up with the moving truck when the other toys have to leave without them.

Remote ride

RC sometimes gives the other toys a ride. Buzz and Woody have both been in the driving seat, but they are powerless to stop RC's batteries draining. If they run out, the ride is over!

Eye-shaped headlights

Rubber tires

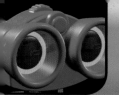

LENNY

A PAIR OF WIND-UP child's binoculars, Lenny is more than just a toy. Thanks to his magnifying lenses he can see further than any of the other toys in Andy's room, which makes him the perfect lookout. Lenny is also small and lightweight enough for the other toys to use and he is always willing to lend his pals a helping eye.

Seeing the truth
Lenny calls it exactly as he sees it. The other toys think that Woody has tossed RC from the moving van, but Lenny sees that the cowboy is actually riding the toy car.

Where's Woody?
When Woody gets mixed up in a yard sale after saving Wheezy, the gang uses Lenny to track him. He is able to give them a close-up of the toy-napper Al McWhiggin.

"He's lighting it! He's lighting it!"

Looking good
Lenny helps the other toys to stay informed about what's going on in the outside world. However, sometimes it's a tough job— when Andy lives next door to Sid, it is Lenny who has to tell the other toys about the gruesome experiments in Sid's yard.

Wind-up handle

Magnifying eyes

Movable feet

MIKE

MULTI-TALENTED MIKE has a number of clever functions including a built-in radio, tape player, and microphone. He is a very useful toy to know! When he's not working, Mike likes to hang out with Mr. Spell. They have electronics in common, after all.

Say it loud
When Woody needs to make his voice heard at toy meetings, he uses Mike's handy built-in microphone.

Mobile Mike
Mike's long, yellow chord allows Woody to walk and talk at the same time. Sometimes it's hard for Mike to keep up with wandering Woody!

Tape player buttons

Radio functions

AM 54 60 80 100 130 160 x10kHz

FM 88 92 96 100 106 108 MHz

ON OFF

Handle for easy carrying

Built-in microphone

PLAYSKOOL

Musical Mike
Mike is more than just Woody's mouthpiece—he has musical talents, too. Whenever the toys want to party, Mike provides the tunes. Wheezy is so pleased with his new squeaker that he bursts into song, and Mike is right there to help him out!

MR. SPELL

MR. SPELL IS a natural teacher. He taught Andy to spell, and also makes an effort to educate the other toys in Andy's room. Mr. Spell runs a series of special awareness sessions for the toys on important subjects, such as the effects of plastic corrosion and what to do if you're swallowed!

Perfectly polite
Mr. Spell gets around by shuffling clumsily from side to side, but his etiquette is perfect. When Woody thanks him for his help, he spells out "You're welcome."

Clever toy
Mr. Spell is no action figure—he's built for educational purposes. But although he's a little square, the other toys respect him for his wide vocabulary and large memory.

Code breaker
When Woody is toy-napped, the gang knows that Al's license plate is a clue. With Mr. Spell's help, Buzz breaks the code.

Did You Know?
Mr. Spell, Wheezy, Etch, Bo Beep, Lenny, RC, and Rocky are all believed to have been sold in the same yard sale.

Computer screen

Alphabetical keypad

TROIKAS

ANDY'S TROIKAS ARE inspired by Russian nesting dolls. These five egg-shaped, wooden toys fit snugly inside each other, in size order, from smallest to biggest. At the first sign of trouble, the trembling troikas jump inside each other so there's only one troika left. Thankfully, it's the fierce looking bulldog troika.

Good egg
The other troikas feel safe inside the biggest one, thanks to his bulldog design, complete with sharp-looking teeth.

Line up
At every team meeting, the troikas obediently get in line, in size order, ready to jump into each other in case of any sudden dangers!

Did You Know?
In Russian, the word "troika" actually means the number three, or three of a kind!

A good fit
The troikas are a close family. Inside the bulldog troika nests a cat troika. The cat troika holds a duck troika, which in turn holds a goldfish. And inside the goldfish there's a cute little ladybug.

Bulldog troika

Cat troika

Goldfish troika

Ladybug troika

Duck troika

MRS. DAVIS

MRS. DAVIS IS a loving Mom to Andy and Molly. She always seems to know just what they like—from great birthday parties and perfect presents to tasty treats at *Pizza Planet*. However, Mrs. Davis is no pushover—she has rules. She expects Andy to be nice to his sister, pick up his toys, and wash his hands occasionally!

Toy fear

Mrs. Davis is a great Mom to Andy, but his toys live in fear that she will either replace them or throw them out. Birthdays and Christmas are particularly stressful times for the toys.

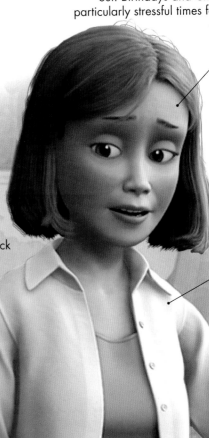

Kind face

Sensible outfit

"I'm sorry, honey, but you know...toys don't last forever."

Clearing out

When Mrs. Davis sees a black garbage bag, she doesn't hesitate in putting it out with the rest of the trash. She doesn't know that it is full of Andy's toys and he had planned on keeping them!

No hoarding

Mrs. Davis encourages her children to look forward and not hang on to too many of their toys. This means there have been plenty of yard sales and donations to places like Sunnyside Daycare over the years.

BONNIE

SWEET-NATURED BONNIE is everything a toy could hope for in an owner, even a toy who has previously been owned and loved by Andy. Kind, exuberant, and with a colorful imagination, Bonnie makes life for her toys great fun.

New owner
Andy is sad to part with his beloved toys, but he knows that giving them to Bonnie is the right thing for all of them. She will take care of them, and, most importantly, she will play with them.

All together
Bonnie has the best collection of toys! She is going to put on some amazing plays with them, as soon as she has decided on the casting...

Pink tutu

New toys
Bonnie can't wait to introduce Andy's toys to her gang. They are going to have some great fun together!

"We have a guest!"

Band aid

Yellow gumboots

To the rescue
Bonnie attends Sunnyside Daycare, but she's not like some of the youngest kids there: Bonnie takes loving care of toys, whether they belong to her or not. She even rescues broken toys, such as Woody, when a trip on a kite leaves him hanging on a tree!

BUSTER

WHEN ANDY GETS a puppy for Christmas, Woody and Buzz just hope that they won't become chew toys. Fortunately, with Buster around, the only danger for the toys is having their paint or parts lovingly licked off, or occasionally being knocked over by the playful pup's enthusiastically wagging tail!

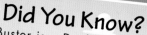

Decoy dog
Buster also has some useful acting skills. When Woody needs to get into the yard, he hangs on Buster's back while the talented dog "acts casual."

Old dog
Like his owner, Andy, Buster eventually grows up. Gone are the days when Buster could give Woody a wild ride around the house. He's barely able to roll over any more.

Collar with name and address tag

Wet nose

Long, wet tongue

Fun and games
One of Buster's favorite games is hide and seek. Woody hides while the rest of the gang try to hold Buster off. Buster then uses his canine nose to seek out his cowboy pal.

House trained
Buster is one smart dog! Woody teaches him to sit up, reach for the sky, and even play dead. Buster also loves to roll over and be tickled. However, he only takes orders from Sheriff Woody. When Andy tries to train him, the clever canine just acts dumb.

SCUD

SID'S MEAN MUTT Scud puts the "terror" into terrier. The horrible hound likes destroying toys as much as his master does. The snarling, growling guard dog patrols the Phillips' house and yard, on the lookout for toys to chew. If it moves, Scud will attack!

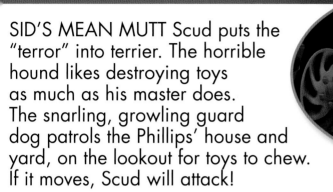

Searching...
Apart from being vicious and suspicious, Scud is also a very determined dog. Defeat is never an option and he will continue to chase anything he can chew.

Small eyes

Chewing...
When Scud finally catches hold of Woody, he doesn't plan on letting go. Fortunately, a traffic pile-up saves Woody from the jaws of doom.

Ugly mutt
Scud looks mean, sounds mean, and he definitely acts mean. He has a white body with brown spots, and a black patch around his left eye. Sid gives him a red spiked collar to complete his menacing look.

Red collar

White body

Did You Know?
Scud is a Bull Terrier, a breed of dog known for their large, egg-shaped heads, and small triangular eyes. They are usually much friendlier than Scud!

BABYHEAD

BABYHEAD IS LEADER of Sid's mutant toys. She is a doll's head attached to spider-like legs made from construction-set pieces. Babyhead lives in the shadows under Sid's bed and creeps around, using her pincers to tap Morse Code out to the other toys to tell them when to come out of hiding.

Misunderstanding
At first, Woody thinks that Babyhead and the mutant toys are as scary as Sid!

Did You Know?
Babyhead's metal claws come in very handy when Sid's experiments go "wrong." Babyhead tries to fix the toys as best as she can.

Hair has been pulled out by Sid

New friends
When Woody realizes the mutant toys are friendly, he enlists their help to save Buzz from Sid. If Woody's plan works, the mutant toys might also find that life becomes sweeter at Sid's house...

Terrified toy
With her empty eye socket, creepy smile, and spider-like movements, Babyhead might look scary, but she is more terrified than terrifying. Years of toy abuse from Sid have taken their toll, but she is actually as gentle as a baby.

One baby-blue eye

Erector-set legs

DUCKY

SQUEAKY DUCKY is another of the mutant toys from Sid's bedroom. With a head from a candy dispenser, a torso from a baby doll, and a springy base, Ducky looks strange but he is tough, fast, and kind of cute. His bizarre combination of parts proves very helpful to Woody when he decides to teach Sid a lesson.

Ring my bell
Woody's rescue plan is brilliant! Ducky, with the help of Legs, has to distract Scud by ringing the doorbell.

Daring duck
Ducky is light with very muscular arms, which makes him the ideal acrobat. He uses both his athletic ability and some bravery when he helps Woody put his plan into action. Danger is water off a duck's back for this cool quacker.

Did You Know?
Ducky is one of the few mutant toys who can make a sound, thanks to his squeaker.

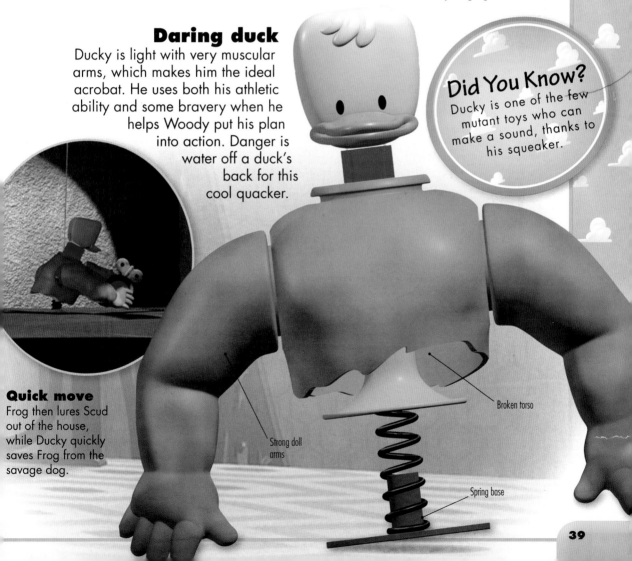

Quick move
Frog then lures Scud out of the house, while Ducky quickly saves Frog from the savage dog.

Strong doll arms

Broken torso

Spring base

HAND-IN-THE-BOX

HAND-IN-THE-BOX drags himself around Sid's bedroom with his fingers, and uses hand signals to communicate. He might look like a monstrosity, but Hand-in-the-Box always jumps at the chance to lend a helping hand to Woody and see the toys finally get revenge on Sid.

Hands up!
When Woody tells the mutant toys his plan, Hand-in-the-Box is on board straight away and shows Woody that he thinks the plan is good.

Monster hand

Helpful hand
Hand-in-the-Box consists of a joke shop monster's hand attached to a Jack-in-the-box spring. He is actually one of Sid's most successful designs—his manual dexterity and spring action come in very handy.

Spring

Top job
In Woody's plan, it is Hand-in-the-Box's job to open the front door after Ducky rings the doorbell. He proves to be a natural!

Box lid

Decorated wooden box

Did You Know?
None of Sid's mutant toys can speak. Whether it is a side effect of Sid's "operations" or just plain fear, no one knows.

LEGS

PART DOLL, PART fishing rod, Legs has an elegant bottom half and a functional top half, with no head. She is a unique combination of length and strength, thanks to her fishing line. Legs looks strange, but she helps Sid to fall hook, line, and sinker for Woody's clever plan.

Reel mechanism

Fishing hook

Rod handle

Reel scary
Sid finally loses his cool when Legs lowers Babyhead onto him. Toys coming to life is too much for the young bully.

Hooking Sid
In Woody's plan, Legs' job is to lower Ducky so that he can ring the doorbell and then she must reel him and Frog to safety.

Gone fishing
There's nothing like a hook, reel, and fishing line to get the tough jobs done. Legs' unique abilities and the strength of her line make her a useful toy to know. She would definitely keep a cool head in a crisis—if she had one.

Elegant shoes

AL MCWHIGGIN

AL IS THE OWNER of *Al's Toy Barn*. This greedy grown-up doesn't like toys because they are fun to play with, he just likes them for the money he can make out of them. He is obsessed with collecting rare toys so he can sell them to museums and make a huge profit.

Fake cheerfulness

Anything for a buck!
Al will do anything he can to get customers to come to *Al's Toy Barn*. He'll even dress up as a chicken if it will make him some bucks!

"You, my little cowboy friend, are gonna make me big buck-buck-bucks!"

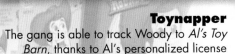

Toynapper
The gang is able to track Woody to *Al's Toy Barn*, thanks to Al's personalized license plate. They just have to crack the code first!

Overweight body

Big phoney
On the outside, Al appears confident and in control, but inside he is a nervous wreck! When he toy-naps Woody from the yard sale, he finds that his stolen treasure is damaged and freaks out.

Did You Know?
Rumor has it that Al wasn't allowed to play with toys as a child, so he makes up for it as an adult by collecting them.

THE CLEANER

KNOWN AS "the Cleaner," this mysterious old man repairs and restores old toys for Al. He can bring even the oldest of toys back to life with painstaking skill, and a very steady hand. Using a minute dab of paint here, a tiny stitch there, or even a new glass eyeball, the Cleaner creates miniature masterpieces.

"Ya can't rush art."

Fixing Woody

The Cleaner not only fixes Woody, but he also retouches his cheeks, paints out a bald spot on his head, and cleans his eyes and ears. His final touch is to paint out Andy's name on his boot.

Sparse gray hair

Smartly dressed

On the case

The Cleaner carries everything he needs inside a specially adapted case. It has dozens of drawers containing paints, spare toy parts, and even a toy treatment chair and bib.

Ancient artist

The Cleaner always concentrates completely on the job in hand and takes great pride in his work. He doesn't care what happens to the toys when he has finished with them, for him it is all about the craft.

Special case

Did You Know?

The Cleaner's real name is Geri. When he is not restoring toys, he likes to relax by playing chess in the park.

CHATTER TELEPHONE

CHATTER TELEPHONE has a permanently happy face, but this pull-along phone is way past his best. He is known as the "Lifer" at Sunnyside because he has been there so long, and witnessed a long line of toys try—and fail—to escape. But Chatter is a tough telephone and he won't let Sunnyside break him.

Phoney smile
Chatter Telephone is always smiling on the outside, but inside he is sad and longs for the day when Sunnyside can be a happy place. When Lotso is ousted, Chatter's smile is finally real.

Time to talk
Chatter is the only toy who dares speak out about Lotso's reign at Sunnyside. He lets Woody know the best way to escape.

"I've been here years, they'll never break me."

Broken phone
Chatter might have seen better days, but he's a tough toy. Even when he is punished by Lotso's thugs for chatting to Woody, he manages to pull through. They can break his receiver, but they can't break his spirit!

Did You Know
Telephones used to look just like Chatter. They had rotating dials, instead of push buttons. Crazy!

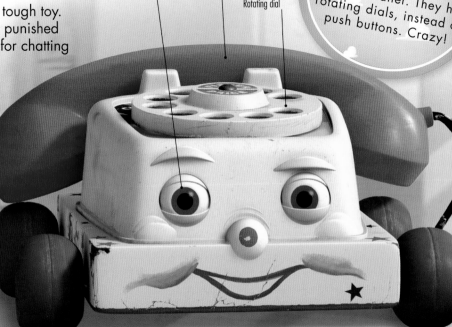

Eyes move up and down

Receiver

Rotating dial

CHUCKLES

THIS SAD CLOWN has had a hard life. His owner, Daisy, accidentally left her favorite toys—Chuckles, Lotso, and Big Baby—at a roadside stop. After that, poor Chuckles had to endure the Caterpillar room and Lotso's reign of terror at Sunnyside. However, sweet Bonnie took pity on his sad eyes and downturned mouth and gave him a new home.

Happy clown
Finally, Chuckles cracks a smile for the first time in years when he sees a drawing of himself by Bonnie.

Sad times
Chuckles sees nothing funny about the situation at Sunnyside and tells Woody some heart-breaking tales about his time there.

"We were lost, cast off, unloved, unwanted."

Rosy cheeks

Humongous clown feet

Clowning about
Chuckles has all the classic clown features: He's got huge clown feet, blue fuzzy hair, thick makeup, and a red nose. The only thing missing is his smile, but now that he lives at Bonnie's he's laughing— on the inside at least.

BIG BABY

BIG BABY IS Lotso's right-hand toy. The monstrous life-size baby doll makes sure that the other toys stick to Lotso's rules. Or else! Big Baby lost his innocence a long time ago—he is covered in ballpoint pen tattoos and one of his baby-blue eyes is broken. However, this broken baby might not be all bad...

"Mama"

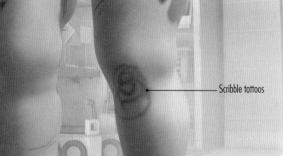

Baby bully
Big Baby used to be owned by a girl named Daisy, along with Lotso and Chuckles. When the three toys were left behind, it left Big Baby feeling vulnerable. Now Big Baby makes other toys feel vulnerable instead.

Growing up
Lotso pushes Big Baby too far by telling him that he is just a baby for still missing Daisy. Big Baby finally has enough—he dumps the selfish teddy in the dumpster and blows him a raspberry!

Fake milk

Cry baby
Lotso lies to Big Baby for his own evil ends: Daisy did care about Big Baby all along. With Lotso gone, Big Baby can remember the good times in peace, and make some new happy memories with his foster parents, Barbie and Ken.

Scribble tattoos

CHUNK

THIS PLASTIC rock monster is one of Lotso's loyal henchtoys. Chunk is covered in protective spikes and has massive fists ready to demolish anything that gets in his way. The mean monster laughs when new arrivals at Sunnyside suffer—he's got a heart of stone.

Play pal
Chunk's oversized, poseable legs make him an excellent toy for the kids at Sunnyside— when he's in friendly mode, that is.

"You think they had a fun playtime?"

Granite gangster
Chunk enjoys teasing the other toys, especially Ken. He likes to annoy the fashion fan by calling him a girls' toy!

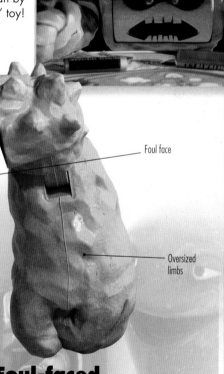

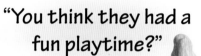

Foul face

Oversized limbs

Foul-faced
Chunk is so two-faced—if the button on the top of his head is pressed, he switches from friendly to foul. Of course, Chunk prefers his mean face, so this is one tough toy you don't want to get on the wrong side of.

SPARKS

THIS ROBOT is programmed to be a mean machine. Sparks has flashing red LED eyes and rolls around Sunnyside on his caterpillar tracks carrying out Lotso's orders. He can also blast sparks from his chest—but don't worry, they are completely safe for children!

Bet on it
Sparks' telescopic arms come in very handy when placing bets in Lotso's secret gambling den.

Play time
With his flashing lights and huge pincers, Sparks is a popular toy with the kids in the Butterfly Room and is never left in the toy box.

Rowdy robot
Sparks' high-tech features make him a versatile villain. His twin caterpillar tracks mean he can move quickly. He can also elevate his body, and he has telescopic arms with painful, pinching pincers.

Flashing red eyes

Elevator action to raise body to new heights

Sturdy rubber wheels

Painful pincers

STRETCH

THIS EIGHT-ARMED purple octopus toy is made from a sticky, gelatinous substance that can withstand extreme stretching. With her glittery body and huge grin, Stretch looks like a fun-loving mollusc, but she is always ready to be the long arm of Lotso's laws. Stretch can use her tentacles to capture any runaway toys.

Always a winner

Stretch always shines at the nightly casino nights held at the gambling den. Unfortunately for her, the winnings are mostly batteries and Stretch isn't battery operated.

"I won. Woo hoo, you lost!"

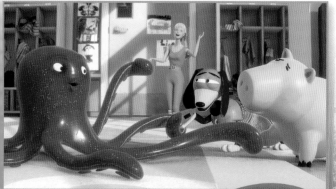

Welcome!

Stretch puts her tentacles to good use, offering a warm, sticky handshake to Barbie, Slinky, and Hamm when they first arrive at Sunnyside. But she's not really friendly—not by any stretch of the imagination.

Girl power

Stretch is the only female in Lotso's gang and she is loyal to her leader right up until the end. However, with Lotso gone, Stretch settles in to the new way of life at Sunnyside and uses her long tentacles to pass messages to Bonnie's new gang.

Friendly face

Sticky suckers

Rubbery leg

TWITCH

BATTLING BUG Twitch just loves to pick a fight. One of Lotso's evil henchtoys, he has a muscle-bound human body, the head of a fly, and huge plastic wings. In fact, he looks like something creepy Sid might have assembled when Andy was a kid!

Laid-back bug
Life is easy for Twitch at Sunnyside. As one of Lotso's henchtoys, he is guaranteed first-class treatment in the workshop spa and his pick of the longlife batteries. He can afford to sit back and relax!

"What do you expect from a girl's toy?"

Battlestaff

Twitch the tease
Twitch considers all toys to be disposable, even the other members of Lotso's gang. He also likes to bug the other toys: He teases Ken about his feelings for Barbie.

Powerful wings

Removable chest armor

Brawny bug
In the new, improved Sunnyside, tough guy Twitch is happy to be played with by the young kids in the Caterpillar Room—as long as he can alternate with his equally tough pal Chunk.

Did You Know?
Twitch's favorite body part is his pecs, but he i pretty proud of his entir warrior physique.

THE BOOKWORM

WITH HIS GLASSES, bow tie, and vest, the Bookworm looks like a harmless brainiac. However, this wriggly villain is the brains of Lotso's gang, maintaining a library of instruction manuals for every toy imaginable. When Lotso wants Buzz to join his gang, he uses Big Baby's brawn and the Bookworm's brains.

Brainy Bookworm
The Bookworm is a green, worm-shaped flashlight. He does nothing but read instruction manuals all day, so he is super smart but not that sociable around the other toys.

Secret knowledge
The Bookworm's library contains valuable information on all the toys at Sunnyside. The Bookworm hands over Buzz Lightyear's manual to Lotso, so that the twisted teddy can reset him to demo mode.

"It was filed under "Lightyear."

Seeing the light
The Bookworm is a bright spark. He realizes that without Lotso around to protect him, he might as well join in the fun. So he does! He even uses his flashlight to light a disco in the Butterfly Room.

Glasses are necessary to see the small print in the instruction manuals

Bright green body

Bright, sturdy flashlight

Crisp, white shirt

BUTTERCUP

BUTTERCUP IS A neatly groomed soft toy unicorn, with a majestic gold horn and fun-to-comb mane and tail. However, underneath his soft and sparkly exterior, this mythical horse is a straight-up, no-nonsense kind of toy who always tells it exactly like it is.

Mythical golden horn

Only kidding!
Buttercup likes to amuse his pals by playing jokes. When Woody arrives at Bonnie's, Buttercup warns him there is no way out! He's just horsing around, of course.

Fun-to-comb tail

Good advice
Buttercup has plenty of acting advice for Woody to help him in Bonnie's role-playing games. Woody makes a promising debut, and he's not even classically trained!

Velvety soft fur

"We do a lot of improv here...you'll be fine."

Buttercup's buddies
Buttercup might be gruff, but he is happy to make friends with Woody and the gang when they arrive at Bonnie's. He's delighted to have a four-legged friend in Bullseye but discovers that he has most in common with the cynical porker, Hamm.

TRIXIE

TRIXIE IS BONNIE'S prehistoric playmate. Made from rigid, durable blue and purple plastic, Trixie is one dinosaur who's never going to be extinct, or even break. Like all Bonnie's toys she is an accomplished actor, and finds that creating a back story helps her to understand her characters better.

Dino diva
Trixie is one talented Triceratops and always gives her very best in Bonnie's games. In her latest role, she has just come back from the doctor with life-changing news!

Prehistoric pals
Rex has always been worried about meeting another dino, but sweet-natured Trixie quickly puts him at ease. The dino duo become great friends and bond over their love of computer games.

"It's just a dinosaur!"

Computer nerd
Trixie is a techno-loving Triceratops. She spends a lot of time on the computer, swapping messages with her dinosaur buddy VelociSTAR237, who lives down the street.

Plastic horn

Movable legs

MR. PRICKLEPANTS

PRICKLY BY NAME, prickly by nature, Mr. Pricklepants is Bonnie's hedgehog toy. The lederhosen-wearing hedgehog is a keen actor and is happiest when he's on stage, delivering crowd-pleasing performances to the other toys.

True friend
Mr. Pricklepants may be a little spiky but he's actually a real softy. He even comes out of character—which is unheard of—to warn Woody that his friends aren't safe at Sunnyside.

Did You Know?
One of Mr. Pricklepants's starring roles is Romeo alongside an Alien playing Juliet in one of Bonnie's games.

"Well, excuse me! I am trying to stay in character."

Jaunty hat

Quiet please
Mr. Pricklepants takes his craft very seriously. It takes immense concentration to stay in character and he has a habit of telling his fellow toys to "Shhh!," earning him the nickname "Baron von Shush."

Star toy
All Bonnie's toys enjoy their daily improvisations, but no one more than Mr. Pricklepants. He just always seems to hog the limelight.

DOLLY

DOLLY IS BONNIE'S stuffed rag doll. With her big eyes, sweet smile, and butterfly clips in her hair, she is as cute as the buttons on her orange polka dot dress. But for some reason, Dolly is often cast as the villain in Bonnie's roleplays. Maybe it's time she got herself an agent!

First impressions
Dolly is happy to welcome any new additions to Bonnie's room and is always willing to impart sound advice to her fellow toys.

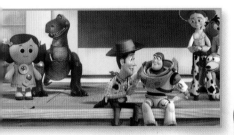

Happy family
With Andy's toys joining the gang, Dolly looks forward to many happy days acting in Bonnie's plays. Maybe one of the new toys can play the villain instead!

"Wow, cowboy. You just jump right in, don't you?"

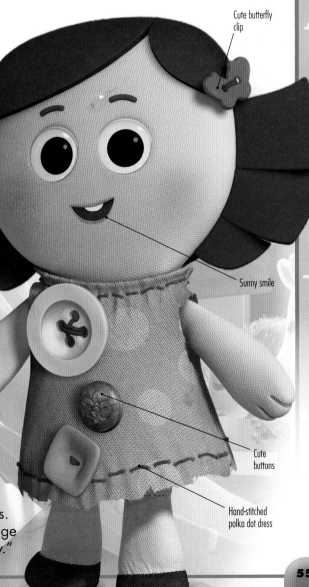

Cute butterfly clip

Sunny smile

Did You Know?
Dolly makes Chuckles smile for the first time since he was abandoned—by showing him onnie's drawing of him smiling.

Down-to-earth doll
On her first meeting with Woody, Dolly suggests he should change his name to something more interesting to succeed in the crazy world of show business. She certainly wishes she had a better stage name than plain old "Dolly."

Cute buttons

Hand-stitched polka dot dress

FLIK

WITH HIS BRIGHT ideas and wacky inventions, Flik is no ordinary ant. But somehow his clever schemes always end in disaster. Tired of slaving for Hopper and his greedy grasshopper gang, Flik steps up to help his colony. He is especially keen to help Princess Atta, whom he adores. However, things don't go according to plan…

Did You Know?

Ants have the largest brains of any insect. Each ant brain has an amazing 250,000 brain cells, and the processing power of a small computer.

Hopeless harvester

Flik builds a grain-gathering gizmo, but it turns out to be a grain-spilling gadget instead! Fortunately, Flik never gives up and soon has a new idea.

Head full of bright ideas

"I was just trying to help."

Spindly legs

Big city: here I come!

Flik is not only inventive, he's also brave. He has the courage to leave Ant Island and go to the city in search of bigger bugs to defend the colony.

Brainy and brave

Flik convinces a troupe of circus bugs to help the ants and comes up with several plans to defeat the grasshoppers. However, when all the plans fail, Flik puts himself in danger to defeat Hopper. Flik's bravery inspires the other ants to be more gutsy, too.

Victory fireworks!

With Hopper defeated, the ants say farewell to the circus bugs by firing grains into the air. It turns out Flik's grain-gathering gizmo does have a use after all!

ATTA

A BORN WORRIER, Princess Atta has a way to go before she is ready to be queen of the colony. In fact, Atta feels totally antsy about the possibility of messing up royally and thinks that Flik is just making her job harder. Her heart is in the right place, though, and she just wants what's best for her subjects.

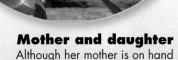

Mother and daughter
Although her mother is on hand for advice, it is time for Atta to make her own decisions. She has to prove that she has what it takes to wear the Queen's crown.

Princess crown made from leaves

Pretty wings

A bug's love
Relieved that the colony is finally safe from the grasshoppers, Atta plants a big kiss on Flik's cheek. It's a dream come true for Flik, and Atta finally realizes that he is the bug for her.

Elegant pose

"The ants pick the food, the ants keep the food, and the grasshoppers leave!"

Learning to lead
As a queen-ant-in-training, Atta takes her responsibilities very seriously—maybe too seriously. Her mother, the Queen, wants her to loosen up. In the end, though, it's Flik's brave example that helps Atta to become a true leader.

DOT

THANKS TO HER tiny name and tiny size, Princess Dot gets teased a lot. She's the smallest member of the Blueberry Scout Troop and the other kids call her "Your Royal Shortness." Luckily, Dot's not short on determination. The little princess has faith in Flik and helps him to believe in himself just when he's ready to give up.

Seeds of change

Flik tells Dot not to worry about being small—tiny seeds grow into giant trees. Later, Dot repeats these words to inspire Flik to return to Ant Island.

"It's payback time, Blueberry style!"

Small but fully grown wings

High flyer

Dot's big frustration is not being able to fly. When she has to bring Flik back to the colony, however, her determination to fly finally takes her up, up, and away!

Fists closed in determination

Did You Know?

Little Dot is almost eaten by a bird, but Flik and the circus bugs save her! The little princess is a precious member of the colony.

Loyal fan

Dot thinks that Flik is the greatest, and that his inventions are super cool. In Dot's eyes, Flik can do no wrong, and her faith in him proves to be 100% on the dot! When Dot's big sister becomes Queen, the little ant inherits her princess tiara.

Short legs

QUEEN

THE QUEEN IS a sensible ruler and a kind, reassuring mother to Atta and Dot. She is also as tough as old boots. Although the Queen is loyal to the old ways, she is willing to try Flik's ideas, as long as they don't put the colony in danger.

Old softy
The Queen never goes anywhere without Aphie, her cute little pet aphid. Maybe being a pet owner is what makes her so relaxed. She certainly loves to spoil Aphie, who adores her and laughs at all her jokes.

Queen's speech
Whether she's welcoming the circus bugs or thanking Flik, the Queen always has just the right words to say.

Elaborate flower crown

"Well, my boy, you came through."

A royal wave

Did You Know?
The Queen helps the circus bugs to trick Hopper by taking part in one of Manny's vanishing tricks!

Royal joker
The Queen has a good sense of humor and a practical view of life. She tells Atta how the grasshoppers come, eat, and then leave. That, she believes, is the ants' lot in life. However, Flik shows her that things can change.

HOPPER

GANG LEADER HOPPER is as mean as they come. With a thick exoskeleton that creaks and rattles like armor, and spiny legs and feet, this big bully towers over the ants. However, Hopper has one major flaw—believing that he is smarter than everyone else.

Hopping mad
Every fall, Hopper and his gang demand an offering from the ants. Thanks to Flik, the ants have no food this year, so the nasty grasshoppers invade the ant hill instead.

Hopper towers over the tiny ants

"It's not about food, it's about keeping those ants in line."

A bug-eat-bug world
Hopper acts tough, but he knows that if the ants ever find out that they outnumber the grasshoppers, they will realize that they don't have to obey them. Hopper does everything in his power to keep the colony afraid of him. He demands that the ants gather up twice as much food before the next leaf falls or, "someone could get hurt."

Bird foo
Flik tries to sca Hopper with a fak bird, but the plan fail So, when Flik lea him to the nest of a re bird, Hopper thin it's another trick until it's too lat

MOLT

SOMETIMES IT'S hard to believe that Molt is Hopper's brother. Hopper always thinks before he speaks, but Molt's mouth doesn't seem to be connected to his brain at all (if he has one, that is). Molt never knows when to shut up, and he can be swayed into thinking just about anything.

Momma's boy
Hopper admits he would have killed Molt long ago, if not for a promise he made to their mother on her deathbed.

"He's quite the motivational speaker, isn't he?"

Bungling brother
Molt's always getting into trouble. His foolish chatter even reveals Hopper's fear of birds to all the ants. He might be stupid, but at least Molt survives to get a job with the circus, while Hopper becomes bird food!

Whoops...
Even flying up and away like the other grasshoppers poses problems for Molt—the clumsy clod hits the ceiling!

Molt's skin is always flaking off

Did You Know?
Molt makes a fresh start by joining P.T. Flea's circus as a strongman. He even gets a new nickname—Tiny!

Strong arms

FRANCIS

TOUGH-TALKING Francis may be a ladybug, but he is no lady! Unfortunately, his beautiful big eyes and pretty wing cases give many circus-goers the wrong idea. Anyone who mistakes this hot-tempered clown for a girl is in for trouble, though.

Stick it to 'em
Francis is devoted to his friend Slim and, as the stick insect cannot fly, carries him on long journeys.

Den mother
Francis finds that he loves spending time with the young ants of Blueberry Troop. He even teaches them how to gamble!

Antenna

Francis has a fierce temper!

Did You Know?
Francis used to play a flower in P.T. Flea's circus but this didn't last long — two flies flirting with him quickly put an end to his budding career!

Polka dot wings

"We are the greatest warriors in all Bugdom!"

Tough talker
In the big city, Francis is ready to fight anyone who suggests he's girlie, but on Ant Island, he gets in touch with his feminine side. When the Blueberry Troop make him an honorary den mother, Francis finally learns that having a soft spot doesn't make him a softie.

HEIMLICH

HEIMLICH IS A mighty munching machine with a big appetite and a big dream—to become a beautiful butterfly. But when Heimlich finally does get his wings, they are too stubby to support his great bulk! Fortunately, happy Heimlich is too easy-going to let that bother him for long.

Fast food
Heimlich never misses an opportunity to tuck into a quick meal. On the way to the ant colony he sneaks in some in-flight snacks.

Heave
It doesn't really matter if Heimlich cannot fly. He has loyal friends to help him along the way.

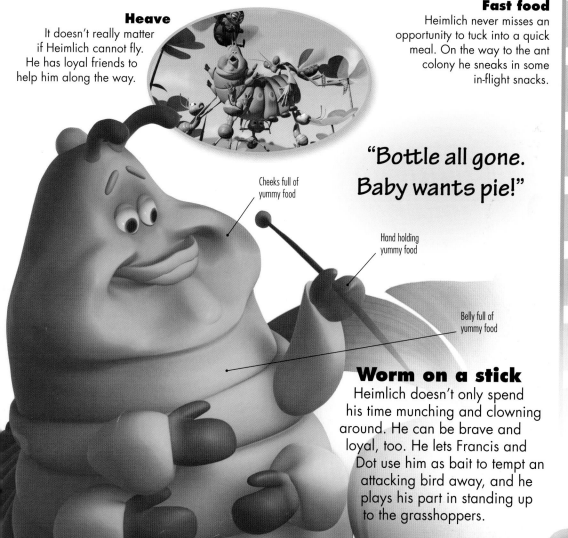

Cheeks full of yummy food

"Bottle all gone. Baby wants pie!"

Hand holding yummy food

Belly full of yummy food

Worm on a stick
Heimlich doesn't only spend his time munching and clowning around. He can be brave and loyal, too. He lets Francis and Dot use him as bait to tempt an attacking bird away, and he plays his part in standing up to the grasshoppers.

MANNY

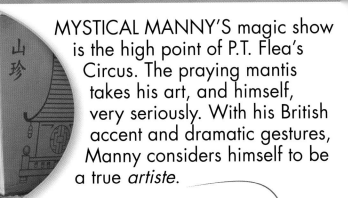

MYSTICAL MANNY'S magic show is the high point of P.T. Flea's Circus. The praying mantis takes his art, and himself, very seriously. With his British accent and dramatic gestures, Manny considers himself to be a true *artiste*.

Insectus transforminus!
Manny's performance includes a transformation act using the Chinese Cabinet of Metamorphosis (a takeaway carton). It's a crowd-pleaser every time.

Crystal balls
Manny and Gypsy's circus skills include pretending to see into the future.

Large eyes

Two pairs of wings

Magic hands

"Yet again it is up to me to rescue the performance."

Kind words
For all his seriousness, deep down Manny is a gentle soul. He finds the right words to soothe Flik when he feels low: "I've made a living out of being a failure," Manny tells Flik. "And you sir—are NOT a failure!"

GYPSY

GYPSY IS MANNY'S wife and his assistant in the circus magic show. When she opens out her gorgeous wings, Gypsy is a real showstopper! However, she is usually happy to stand back and let her husband, Manny, take center stage.

Colorful wings

Upturned nose

Off to Ant Island!
Gypsy is like a mother to the circus troupe. She often acts as their spokesbug.

"Sh! He's in a trance."

Slender legs

Amazing moth
Gypsy may look delicate, but she's not just lovely, she's brave too. She flies in and flashes her wings to distract the creek bird when it is attacking Heimlich. And she refuses to tell Hopper how she and Manny have "magicked away" the Queen during their transformation act.

Did You Know?
Female gypsy moths are usually bigger than males, but many of them cannot fly.

Wise wife
Gypsy works hard helping Manny outside the circus ring as well as in it. Manny's head is so far up in the clouds, there's no telling how he'd ever manage without Gypsy's sensible guidance.

DIM

FLIK'S FIRST SIGHT of Dim, the rhinoceros beetle, leaves him in no doubt that he's found a troupe of truly tough bugs. But despite his scary-looking horn and thundering size, Dim is a total sweetie, who wouldn't hurt a fly.

Did You Know?
Rhinoceros beetles are so-named because of their large horns. However, they cannot bite or sting, so are harmless to humans.

Super-strong wings

Safe flight
Dim's superior wing power allows him to airlift Dot, Tuck, and Roll out of danger during the bird attack.

Large horn

The bugmobile
Dim may not be the brainiest bug, but he is dependable. His strength and size mean he also acts as the troupe's transportation. On Ant Island he makes himself useful and popular by giving the young ants rides.

Tender trainer
Rosie is Dim's trainer, but sometimes she is more like a mother to him. She looks after Dim and soothes him when he's hurt.

"Dim don't wanna go."

TUCK AND ROLL

NO INSECT CAN match this pair of crazy pill bugs when it comes to acrobatics and gymnastic feats. Tuck and Roll spend all their time tucking, rolling, somersaulting, flipping, and tumbling with tremendous zest.

Ta-dah!
Tuck and Roll act as cannonballs in P.T. Flea's circus troupe. With their wonky smiles and waving legs, the pill bug pair end each routine with a flourish.

"You fired! You fired!"

Did You Know?
Tuck pulls off one of Hopper's antennas and uses it in the troupe's final show!

Baffled bugs
Tuck and Roll are from Hungary. Flik chatters to them non-stop all the way to Ant Island, without realizing that they don't understand a word of English.

Tuck wears a slightly crazed expression

Roll has a unibrow

Hopper's antenna

Pill bugs have eight legs

Tough twins
Tuck and Roll are a hot-tempered duo. They are always arguing and hitting each other. To onlookers, their squeaky squabbling is more entertaining than their tumbling. Even Hopper thinks it's funny.

P.T. FLEA

GREEDY CIRCUS owner and ringmaster P.T. Flea will do anything for money, including getting burned alive in the name of entertainment! The fiery flea spends most of his time yelling at his troupe, as they lurch from one disaster to another. Finally, he fires them!

Flea finale
The circus' "Flaming Death" finale begins with P.T. holding a lit match. It ends with his body being burned to a frazzle. The audience loves it!

"They're gonna make me rich."

Ka-ching!
With a surprise hit on his hands, P.T. Flea tracks down the troupe and tries to win them back.

Greedy eyes

Money-hungry mouth

Did You Know?
P.T. Flea returns from the ant colony with a bigger and better circus, now including a troupe of acrobatic ants!

Money grabber
P.T. Flea is a parasite, who squeezes money out of the low-lives that visit his big top. If audiences complain that the show stinks, P.T.'s answer is simple: "No refunds after two minutes." His dream is to make the circus a moneymaking success.

Singed legs

Flammable body

THUMPER

SNARLING THUMPER is less like a grasshopper and more like a mad guard dog. When Hopper doesn't get his way, he uses Thumper as a threat. Vicious and unpredictable, Thumper has to be kept on a leash—and even then it takes two handlers to control him!

a bug's life

Mean eyes

Menacing expression

Bad grasshopper!

Scary Thumper enjoys nothing more than terrifying others. But when the tables are turned, he reveals himself to be a complete coward. A smack from Dot and a roar from Dim is all it takes to make Thumper go from ferocious to frightened to fleeing in seconds!

Fierce hands

Mighty muscle
Wherever Hopper is, Thumper isn't far behind, ready to do some damage.

Size isn't everything
When the ants try to chase the grasshoppers away, Dot runs into Thumper. But the tough grasshopper gets more than he bargained for when he takes on determined Dot!

"Screech! Screech! Screech!"

69

SLIM

SARCASTIC AND A bit pessimistic, stick insect Slim has a fragile ego that is easily broken when people laugh at him. The problem is that he's a clown, so when an audience is laughing, it means that he has done a good job!

Stuck for words
Slim thinks he has star quality, but he is usually cast as a broom, a stick, or a flower. Performing a "Spring flowers" routine with Francis is not his idea of show business!

"Francis, you're making the maggots cry."

Long, stick-like head

A way out
Slim is quick to accep Flik's offer to trave to Ant Island. H thinks it will be th perfect escap from a grou of flies who ar after Francis

Long, stick-like body

Long, stick-like fingers

A friend indeed
Although he hates being laughed at, Slim reckons there's one good thing about being a clown—his fellow clowns. He's especially close to the tough ladybug, Francis, who carries Slim around by tucking him under a wing.

ROSIE

BLACK WIDOW spider Rosie is glamorous, talented, and hardworking. At the circus, she is mistress of the high wire and Dim's trainer. Rosie is a real team player and always ready to help out the rest of the troupe.

Misunderstanding
Like the rest of the troupe, at first Rosie doesn't understand what Flik is asking of them. She thinks he's a talent scout!

"Come on everyone. Break a leg!"

Spider skills
Rosie can weave a web so fast it makes your head spin—a skill that's useful when rescuing her friends from sticky situations. She can cast out a lifesaving line in record time—or use her silken thread to tie up an annoying busybody, such as P.T. Flea.

Rosie's role
In the "Flaming death" routine, Rosie's job is to spin the line that will save Tuck and Roll.

Stylish purple eyeshadow

Kind expression

Eight long legs

71

SULLEY

JAMES P. SULLIVAN, known as Sulley, is the top Scarer at Monsters, Inc., a company that provides energy to the city of Monstropolis by capturing the screams of children from the human world. Sulley might be fierce on the Scare Floor, but off it he's as friendly as he is furry.

Dream team
Sulley and his best pal Mike are extremely close. They live together, work together, and even went to school together. Surprisingly, the firm friends hardly ever argue.

Shaggy green and purple fur

"Hey...may the best monster win."

New pal
The monsters believe that human kids are highly toxic and dangerous. At first, Sulley is scared of Boo. But the gentle giant soon grows so fond of her that he finds a new way to power Monstropolis without scaring anyone—using children's laughter!

Modest monster
Sulley is an A-list celebrity around Monstropolis, but he doesn't let fame go to his furry head. Sulley treats everybody the same, whether they're co-workers or monsters. He's just a regular guy!

MIKE

FAST-LIVING AND FUN-LOVING, Mike is Sulley's Scare Assistant and best pal. He is a real ball of energy. You won't find Mike staying in and watching TV—unless it's to see himself in the new Monsters, Inc. commercial.

Monster love
Mike and his "Shmoopsie Poo" Celia only have an eye for each other. He treats her to dinner on her birthday and supplies her with an endless stream of compliments, which she loves.

Monsters, Inc. hard hat

Take the mike, Mike
When Monsters, Inc. changes from scaring kids to making them laugh, Mike puts his comedic skills to the test. Mike even resorts to swallowing his mic to make a child laugh. His jokes definitely need a little more work...

"Nothing is more important than our friendship."

Round body

Monster mouth
Quick-witted Mike has a smart line for everyone and everything. Sometimes his big green mouth gets him into trouble, but his quick wit usually gets him out of even the stickiest situation.

Did You Know?
Mike has always suffered from poor eyesight. He gets his lenses from the upmarket Cyclops Optical. Well, when you've just got one eye, only the best will do!

RANDALL BOGGS

RANDALL BOGGS IS slimy, slippery, and disgusting—and that's just his personality. The meanest monster around, he's Sulley's main rival at Monsters, Inc. Randall is challenging Sulley for the position of top Scarer, but one thing's for sure, he'll never win any popularity prizes!

Crafty expression

Secret plan
Randall has created a top secret scream-extracting machine and he plans to test it on a human child. But until he finds one, Mike the monster will have to do!

Lots of teeth

She's behind you!
The horrible monster isn't prepared for brave two-year-old Boo to stop his despicable plans! He's certainly met his match in the tiny tot.

Sneaky hand gesture

On the prowl
Repugnant Randall is a color-changing chameleon who can make himself almost invisible. The creep then creeps around scaring children and annoying his rival monsters.

Lizard skin

WATERNOOSE

PROUD, PROPER, AND pretty scary, Henry J. Waternoose is the boss of Monsters, Inc. The company has been in the Waternoose family for three generations, and Henry J. began his illustrious career on the Scare Floor when he was a young monster (a long time ago).

Star pupil
Waternoose is proud of his top Scarer, Sulley, and often uses his super scare skills to show other monsters' how it's done.

"I'll kidnap a thousand children before I let this company die!"

Horrible Henry
Waternoose pretends to take care of Boo, but really he is planning to extract screams from her with the horrible scream extracting machine!

Fake facade
Underneath his professional exterior, Waternoose is actually dishonest and devious. He is facing a looming scream shortage and is under intense pressure to get his employees to collect more screams. He will do anything to make his company profitable again, even if it means betraying loyal friends like Sulley.

Smart tuxedo

Crab-like legs

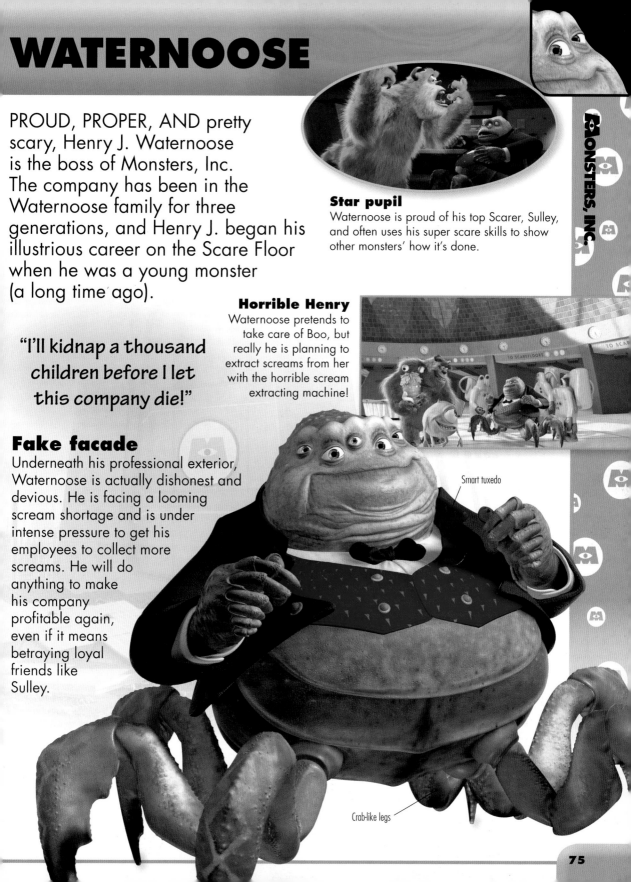

CELIA

MONSTERS, INC.

AS THE RECEPTIONIST at Monsters, Inc., Celia has learnt to be super-efficient. She has to greet visitors, answer the phones, and make announcements over the intercom—sometimes all at the same time! It's a pity the five snakes on her head can't help her out.

Purple snake-hair

Fashionable fur collar

Scaly shift dress

Mad monster
When Celia and the five snakes on her head get cross, Monstropolis had better watch out! Seeing that her Googly Bear—Mike—and Sulley are trying to escape from Randall, she makes sure she stops the horrible monster from catching them.

"Oh, Googly-woogly, you remembered!"

Long, elegant tentacles

Concise Celia
Celia has a no-nonsense approach in and out of the office. Although she loves a romantic night out with the apple of her eye, Mike, Celia keeps him on his six toes. If she senses that he is keeping secrets from her, she demands to know the truth—immediately!

True love
Celia and Mike are a match made in monster heaven. Although Mike sometimes makes her mad, she wouldn't change a thing about him.

ROZ

DISPATCH MANAGER FOR Scare Floor F, Roz is a stickler for the rules. Just one dirty look from this stern-looking giant slug is enough to make all the Scare Assistants tremble with fear, particularly if they haven't handed in their paperwork on time.

Permanent scowl

Sharp-eyed slug
This sly slug is bossy and conscientious for a reason! As leader of the CDA (Child Detection Agency) she worked undercover at Monsters, Inc. to expose the scandal at the company.

No sweet talking here!
Roz is immune to sweet talk—no matter how hard the assistants try, they just can't shift her permanent frown. There's more to Roz than scowls and sarcasm, however, and she always seems to know exactly what's going on at Monsters, Inc…

"I'm watching you Wazowski, always watching."

Slimy slug body

BOO

BOO IS ONLY two years old, but she is very brave. The plucky youngster is not afraid to hang out with a bunch of the weirdest looking oddballs you can find. Boo has a limited vocabulary of about three words, but she has loads of energy and laughs at the most unexpected things, including her monster friends!

No more tears
Boo has a massive effect on the monster Sulley and the whole of Monstropolis. Thanks to her influence, laughter rather than screams now fuel the city.

Monster disguise
When Boo gets lost in the Monsters, Inc. factory, she tags along with a group of young monsters being shown around the factory. Her monster costume helps her to blend right in.

"Boo!"

Fake hair

Plastic tentacles

Did You Know?
One of Boo's favorite toys is her Jessie Yodeling Cowgirl doll

Here Kitty, Kitty
Boo is a very curious child and she loves to go exploring. This causes some stress for Sulley, her favorite monster and friend. Boo thinks he looks like a giant pussycat and calls him "Kitty."

BOMINABLE SNOWMAN

THE ABOMINABLE SNOWMAN is more amiable than abominable. He's been exiled to the Himalayas for many years, but he isn't complaining. He loves his "winter wonderland," where he can sip a mug of yak's milk in his cozy cave. When Sulley and Mike are banished here by Waternoose, Abominable gives them a warm, Yeti welcome!

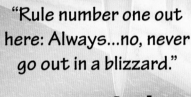

Sad Sulley
Despite the Yeti's enthusiastic greeting, Sulley can't help but miss Boo. He comes up with a plan to return to Monstropolis and rescue his favorite youngster.

Sweet treat
Abominable adores lemon-flavored snowcones and kindly offers the sweet snacks to his guests. However, Mike is more interested in keeping warm!

"Rule number one out here: Always...no, never go out in a blizzard."

Cool guy
The snowman is a friendly giant and always gives travelers a warm welcome in a cold climate. The hospitable Yeti offers shelter from blizzards and an endless supply of lemon-flavored snowcones.

Thick fur to keep warm in chilly climate

Abominable is an extremely happy Yeti!

Did You Know?
Abominable loves his home in the Himalayas so much that he has no plans to return to the human world.

GEORGE

GEORGE IS ONE of the most laid back monsters on the Scare Floor. Easygoing and popular, he isn't too bothered about being the best. George would much rather take it easy with the other Scarers and share a joke or two on the Scare Floor than be top of the Scarer Leaderboard.

Contamination
Trouble seems to follow poor George everywhere. When a kid's sock gets stuck to his furry back, the CDA is called immediately to catch the contaminated monster. George has a very close shave and loses most of his shaggy fur!

Mild monster

Some might say that George is a little too carefree and, consequently, this accident-prone monster often gets into scrapes. George is good friends with Mike and Sulley and they often hang out together on the Scare Floor.

George's horn

Did You Know?
George starred as himself in th play *Put That Thing Back Wher it Came From or So Help Me*, written, directed, and produce by Mike Wazowski.

Big, baby-blue eyes

Tufts of fur

Cone to stop George scratching his freshly shaved skin

CLAWS

PETE "CLAWS" WARD has the largest, sharpest claws on the Scare Floor and he's proud of it! Each morning, Claws lovingly extends his talons to their full, terrifying length, ready for a great day of scaring.

Dinner time
After a hard day's work on the Scare Floor, Claws enjoys nothing more than getting his claws into a spot of sushi at *Harryhausen's* restaurant with his monster pals.

Little horns

Big softy
Claws isn't actually as fierce as he looks. Nearly being touched by a child can reduce him to a big, blubbering blue mess.

Officially the sharpest claws at Monsters, Inc.

Razor-sharp teeth

ort, spiky

Short legs

Did You Know?
Claws is close friends with fellow Scarers George and Nick "Lanky" Schmidt.

FUNGUS

GEEKY THREE-EYED Fungus has the terrifying task of being Randall's Assistant. His career may have blossomed with Randall's success, but the experience has made Fungus into a nervous monster. Secretly, he'd rather be inventing crafty contraptions than pandering to the loathsome lizard.

Always on call
Fungus is clever and hardworking—well, he has to be, working for a demanding monster like Randall!

Eyes wide open
Keeping Randall happy can be a terrifying business, and keeping his evil agenda secret is equally scary. Fungus has to keep all three eyes open, just in case something goes wrong.

Three-eyed spectacles

Official Monsters, Inc. pass

Important Monsters, Inc. documents

Did You Know?
After Randall is banished to th human world, Fungus starts a n career making kids laugh for Monsters, Inc.

JERRY

AS THE FLOOR manager at Monsters, Inc. Jerry ensures everything runs flawlessly on the Scare Floor. Luckily, Jerry is an organized guy, so panicking monsters, shredded doors, and contamination scares don't fluster him. He works hard to make sure that the maximum amount of screams is captured every day.

Scare challenge
Working on the Scare Floor is a challenge, but this doesn't frighten Jerry—in fact, he relishes his role as manager!

3-2-1-action!
Jerry counts down the seconds left for the monsters to get to work and start scaring.

"We may actually make our quota today!"

All-rounder
Jerry has learned to deal with all the monstrous egos on the Scare Floor and he is regarded as a key employee at Monsters, Inc. He even has a speaking part in the firm's TV commercial.

Did You Know?
Jerry has seven fingers on each hand—handy when he's doing countdowns for the monsters!

NEEDLEMAN

MONSTERS, INC.

Did You Know?
Needleman plays Randall Boggs in Mike's play, *Put That Thing Back Where It Came From Or So Help Me.*

NERDY NEEDLEMAN IS the company janitor, along with his best pal, Smitty. This odd pair do lots of small but essential jobs, such as pushing carts of scream canisters, operating the door-shredding machine, and straightening out pictures... well, somebody has to!

Monster fans
Needleman and Smitty are the monsters' biggest fans, and their hero is Sulley. Whenever he speaks to them, they erupt into a fit of nervous giggles.

Big red nose

"Quiet! You're making him lose his focus."

A dirty job
Needleman and Smitty are a great team. They love their janitor jobs, even if the work is sometimes dirty—after all, they get to mingle with A-list celebrities like Sulley.

Skinny arms

Long, slim body

Monsters, Inc. cleaning rota

Not so needle sharp
Needleman isn't the sharpest monster in the factory. However, he makes up for this with lots of enthusiasm, and he's a valued member of the Monsters, Inc. team.

SMITTY

WITH HIS BAD HAIRCUT and wonky helmet, Smitty looks awkward and clumsy—and unfortunately his looks don't lie! Together with fellow clumsy caretaker Needleman, the hare brained pair stumble and bumble their way around the factory carrying out various tasks.

Official Monsters, Inc. hard hat

Not on the ball

Needleman and Smitty have low concentration spans and often don't pay attention to the job at hand. They very nearly throw Boo into the garbage crusher!

Smitty needs a haircut!

Monster hero

It's hard for Smitty to contain his excitement when Sulley says hello to him. He respects the furry monster so much, he insists on calling him Mr. Sullivan.

Hard worker

Smitty is smitten with the stars of the Scare Floor, like Sulley—he thinks they are sooo cool. Smitty is a great monster to have around the place—he has a big heart and is always helpful.

Did You Know?

Smitty and Needleman sometimes quarrel. Needleman gets especially annoyed with Smitty when he fails to say Sulley's name correctly!

BILE

THADDEUS BILE, KNOWN as Phlegm to his friends, is a trainee Scarer. He's a popular monster with the other trainees, mainly because he's just as useless as they are! Bile has a lot to learn if he's going to make it onto the payroll...

Fail!
Bile's botched attempt at scaring in the Simulator Room doesn't impress the boss, Waternoose. Going for a "snake-slash-ninja" approach just isn't going to cut it at Monsters, Inc. no matter how much hissing Bile throws in for good measure!

A lot to learn
Bile needs to learn to work on looking terrifying rather than terrified! In the Simulator Room, a robotic child makes the rookie recruit jump so much, Bile ends up in a heap on the floor.

"Uh, my friends call me Phlegm."

CHARLIE

CHARLIE IS GEORGE Sanderson's Assistant on the Scare Floor. With two protruding eyes on stalks, he is great at spying trouble. Unfortunately, Charlie's tentacles are a little trigger-happy—he calls the Child Detection Agency at the slightest sign of a problem.

2319!

Charlie likes to be in the center of the action at Monsters, Inc. He can often be heard shouting "2319" at the first sign of trouble. This is the code for an emergency, and makes the CDA come running.

Eyes on stalks always on the lookout for trouble

Did You Know?
Charlie manages to make it safely back from the Himalayas.

On the ball
Charlie is a very conscientious employee, but this has created problems for his clumsy friend George. Calling in the CDA has resulted in George ending up on crutches with all his fur shaved off!

Banished!
Charlie gets on well with George, and the two firm friends always have fun working in the factory. But George is a little tired of visits from the CDA, and before Charlie can make another call, George pushes him through a door to the Himalayas!

Three tentacle legs

WAXFORD

WAXFORD IS AUGUSTUS "Spike" Jones' Assistant. He is, without a doubt, one of the shiftiest-looking monsters in the factory, but that's because he has five very large eyeballs on stalks. Waxford isn't shifty at all; in fact he is perfectly trustworthy, always keeping an eye—or five—on what's going on.

Did You Know?
Waxford has tentacles instead of feet.

Five shifty-looking eyes

Shift the blame
Looking as shifty as Waxford means that he often gets the blame for things he hasn't even done!

Eye eye
Waxford might have five eyes but he's not as sharp-eyed as Roz. No one is.

Scaly skin

Tree trunk
When he's standing up, Waxford looks a little bit like a tree that's wearing five helmets. As Spike's Assistant, the helmets are a necessary precaution to protect him from Spike's needle-sharp spines.

Tentacles

MRS. NESBITT

MRS. NESBITT IS probably the least scary monster at Monsters, Inc. (well, apart from Claws, maybe). She runs the Monsters, Inc. school for young monsters with a perfect balance between firmness and understanding. Having four arms means the plump purple-spotted monster can easily comfort more than one child at a time.

All monsters allowed
Mrs. Nesbitt welcomes all monsters in her class. However, she might want to take a closer look at the purple "monster" with the eyes on stalks...

Teacher's pets
All the mini monsters love Mrs. Nesbitt. Although they can misbehave sometimes, they think she's a class act and the perfect teacher to keep an eye on them...although her eyesight might need to be tested!

Did You Know?
Mrs. Nesbitt has worked at Monsters, Inc. as a teacher since the company first opened.

Sensible hairstyle

Squishy body perfect for giving monster hugs

NEMO

THIS BRIGHT LITTLE clownfish knows very little about the big bad ocean out there. He has a doting dad who doesn't let him stray far from the cozy anemone they call home. Young Nemo is the least prepared of all the sea creatures for the adventure he finds himself plunged into!

"Does anyone know where my dad is?"

Dad knows best
Nemo's dad, Marlin, looks after his son with great care. He always tells him that he can't swim as well as other fish because of his small right fin. This only makes Nemo eager to prove himself.

White stripes make Nemo harder for hungry predators to spot

In the tank
Nemo is scared of the Tank Gang at first. However, he soon learns that they are all lovable in their own weird ways.

Lucky fin

Caught!
Nemo isn't the fastest fish around, but he makes up for it with a heroic spirit. Taken to a fish tank in Sydney, Australia, Nemo is soon making new friends and realizing that he can survive without his dad fussing over him.

Nemo uses his tail to push himself along

DORY

A CRAZY OPTIMIST with a big heart, this bubbly blue fish is Marlin's best hope for finding his son. Just one tiny problem—Dory's short-term memory makes her forget what she is doing every few minutes. Still, she is happy to help search for Bingo, or Harpo, or whatever his name is...

Big eyes to see in murky places

Down with the kids
Dory is a natural with kids, and turns Marlin into a legend of the seas when she tells the young turtle dudes all about his incredible adventures.

Squishy surprise
Dangerous jellyfish are just big bouncy trampolines to Dory, who can't help seeing the fun in everything.

"I think I lost somebody, but I can't remember."

Regal tangs start out life yellow

Fin to zoom around really fast

Deep Dory
Dory is loaded with hidden talents. She can read human, even when about to be eaten by an anglerfish. She can also speak whale, which comes in very handy when you're trapped inside one. When faced with the unknown her motto is: "Just keep swimming."

Did You Know?
Dory is a regal tang. These fish have a powerful smell and can be poisonous, causing sickness and headaches if eaten.

MARLIN

MEET THE MOST over-protective parent in the ocean. Marlin was just another wise-cracking clownfish until a barracuda ate his wife and left him with just one egg to raise. Now he has promised that nothing will ever happen to his son. But that's the problem—he has to learn to let Nemo live a little!

"I didn't come this far to be breakfast!"

Letting go
Nemo's first day at school is a huge challenge—not for Nemo, but for his dad. In fact, Marlin would be happy to put the day off for another few years, just to be on the safe side!

A special layer of goo protects clownfish from anemone stings

Large eyes on the lookout for danger

Mighty Marlin
Marlin becomes the most famous fish in the sea when he braves every danger—from sharks to seagulls—to find his son. Along the way he learns to trust others and even gets slightly better at telling jokes!

Reunited
Marlin is the happiest dad in the world when he finds his son again. Nemo just wants to tell his dad he never really hated him!

CORAL

WITH A NEW home on the reef, a sea view, and several hundred babies on the way, Coral seemed to have a sweet life in store for her. That is until the dark day a big barracuda stopped by for dinner. In a terrible attack, Coral's dreams turned into a nightmare.

The name game
When Coral and Marlin visit the cozy hideaway of their big clutch of eggs, the only problem they can foresee in life is finding names for all of them.

id You Know?
Clownfish produce anywhere from one hundred to a thousand eggs.

"There's over 400 eggs, odds are, one of them is bound to like you."

Tail fin (personal rudder)

Hopeful expression

Hatching Nemo
Sadly, just one of Coral's eggs survives the terrible barracuda attack. Tiny Nemo keeps happy memories of Coral alive for Marlin.

Courageous Coral
Coral showed amazing courage in trying to protect her family, but she was gobbled up along with her eggs—well, all except one. The sole survivor was cherished by the heartbroken Marlin, and given a name that Coral liked: Nemo.

MR. RAY

LEARNING AT FISH school is always fun with Mr. Ray in charge. Cheerful and popular, he's a great asset to the school, and he is both teacher and school bus. The pupils enjoy the daily game of hiding from Mr. Ray—under his own wings!

Did You Know?
Rays are related to sharks and are known to be intelligent creatures.

School rules
Mr. Ray gets on swimmingly with all the youngsters in his care. However, he does insist that, when he gives them a lift, they don't stick gum under the seats!

"Welcome explorers! So much to see, so much to learn."

Class trip
Since the whole reef is Mr. Ray's schoolroom, every day is a class trip to see some new wonder of the deep.

White dots help rays to hide in sand on the sea floor

Wing-like fins for gliding through water

Ray of light
Mr. Ray thinks of his charges not just as students, but as fellow undersea explorers. When teaching, he uses catchy rhymes to get across key facts: "Seaweed is cool, seaweed is fun, it makes its food from the rays of the sun!"

SHELDON, TAD, PEARL

NEMO'S CLASS IS made up of all kinds of reef fish. The children all seem to get along, but Mr. Ray has two strict rules that the students must follow: Learn and have fun! On his first day at school, Nemo makes three new friends.

Sheldon could sneeze at any moment

"Awwww! You guys made me ink!"

Dare scare
The three friends are dismayed when they lose their new friend Nemo on day one. A game of "touch the butt" (meaning the bottom of a boat) goes seriously wrong.

Sheldon
Sheldon is H_2O intolerant, so water makes him sneeze. That's an embarrassing problem for an ocean dweller!

Did You Know?
Unlike most species, the male seahorses, not the females, give birth to babies!

False "eyespot" fools predators

Tad
Tad the butterfly fish gets bored if he isn't the center of attention. He often makes trouble in class and has to stay back and clean the eraser sponges.

Like any octopus, Pearl inks when excited or frightened

Pearl
This sweet little flapjack octopus has a small problem—when she gets excited she squirts out ink. This might lead to a bit of teasing at school, but one day this skill could save Pearl's life from predators.

GILL

THE MOODY MASTERMIND of the Tank Gang, this Moorish idol fish believes that his kind were never meant to live in a box. From his lair in the plastic skull, Gill constantly dreams of freedom. He is never short of an escape plan—no matter how crazy and dangerous it is.

Thin body for slipping in among the crannies of coral reefs

Did You Know?
Moorish idol fish have colorful stripes, which help them to hide in the reef.

"All drains lead to the ocean, kid."

The mastermind
When Nemo arrives, Gill senses a promising new recruit and gives the clownfish a nickname: Sharkbait. Gill puts Nemo in peril with his daring plans, but when it really counts the wily leader risks his life to set his friend free.

On the lookout
Gill may lie low most of the time, but his brilliant mind is always scheming. A deep thinker, he knows that all drains lead to the sea—and freedom.

BLOAT

BLOAT LOOKS LIKE any regular fish—until he gets mad, that is. When this short-tempered blowfish blows his cool, he puffs up into a spiky ball of rage. When Bloat was little, his big brother used to use him as a football, which just made him madder!

Fit to burst
Even Gill stands well back when Bloat gets excited—after all, the fish never know when their pal might explode with anger.

Brother bloat
Bloat puffs up with pride when he is given the big role in the Tank Gang ritual at Mount Wannahockaloogie.

Fins used for flapping

Did You Know?
Blowfish are able to inflate because they have elastic skin and no ribs!

Spines are poisonous

"You must pass through the Ring of Fire."

Ball of energy
Bloat's inflatable body is useful in an emergency and he uses it to knock over the plastic volcano in one of Gill's escape attempts. The blowfish is an expert on extreme fish and master of ceremonies at the Ring of Fire initiation ceremony.

GURGLE

RAISED IN A run-down pet shop, Gurgle the royal gramma fish was covered in so much slime he thought he was green. After being sold, Gurgle was very grateful to the cleaner shrimp Jacques for revealing his true colors. Since then, Gurgle has sworn never to get his fins dirty again.

"I think you're nuts."

Neurotic fin-in-mouth gesture

Tank talk
There are two topics of conversation in the tank, dentistry and escape. Gurgle always lets the bigger fish talk first

Colorful character
Gurgle's rainbow colors reflect his feelings. When he's anxious he turns a fetching shade of blue. Scummy slime and dangerous Darla are the two things guaranteed to have this effect on him.

Royal gramma fish are known for their rainbow colors

Fine fish
A fish of finer feelings, Gurgle is reluctant to get too close to a real-life reef fish like Nemo. He is also quick to show his disgust at the escape plan that involves everyone making the water in the tank filthy.

PEACH

THIS SHARP-EYED starfish makes the perfect lookout, because she enjoys being in one place for a long time. Peach likes to count how many cups of coffee the dentist drinks, so the fish can guess his next bathroom break and carry out their escape plans while he's away.

Star spy
Peach watches every move the dentist makes and can be relied upon to relay the latest hot news from the surgery to the trivia-hungry Tank Gang.

"Shhhh! He's coming!"

Sticking with it
Tiny suckers all over Peach's body guarantee super stickability. She's just as happy resting on a wall as on the ground.

Beady eyes always on the lookout

Suckers grab hold of surfaces

Big sister
Sensitive Peach looks out for new arrival Nemo as if he is a younger brother—protesting when he is sent on a mission to jam the tank's revolving fan. She even worries about him in the frankly phony Ring of Fire ceremony—well, the volcano is plastic!

Did You Know?
If a starfish's arm is cut off, it will grow back again within a year!

THIS HUMBUG FISH never feels lonely because she is convinced that her reflection is her identical twin sister! Deb finds Flo to be a loyal companion who is always there when she needs her. Her "sister" is never loud and is always in tune with her moods.

Jealous guys
Friends come round to visit Deb, but none of them seem to speak to Flo. Deb doesn't mind though—the tank guys are all just jealous of the special friendship she has with her twin!

Blue and white stripes

Deb's reflection (but don't tell her!)

Big eyes

"Don't listen to anything my sister says, she's nuts!"

In my face
There are a couple of drawbacks to having such an in-your-face friend. For a start, Flo sometimes blocks the view when Deb wants to look outside the tank. Deb also warns people to ignore whatever Flo says—as she's nuts!

JACQUES

BEYOND COMPARE IN the field of personal grooming, this classy cleaner shrimp maintains the highest standards of cleanliness. Jacques once belonged to the President of France, who gave him as a gift to the Australian Prime Minister, who then passed him on to the dentist.

Did You Know?
In the ocean, cleaner shrimp "clean" fish by eating the tiny animals who live on their bodies!

"I am ashamed."

Large eyes always on the lookout for specks of dirt

Helmet home
Jacques lives in this antique diver's helmet, which is not only a cozy home, but an escape from the scummy world outside and his disappointingly slimy friends.

Jacques' helmet home

Magic touch
To Monsieur Jacques, cleaning isn't just a job—it's an art. When working on a new client, he really puts on a show and displays all the style and showmanship of a stage conjurer.

Long time no sea
Despite being named after the famous ocean explorer Jacques Cousteau, Jacques has never actually been in the real ocean. However, he considers this his good fortune—after all, the sea has no state-of-the-art filter system!

Squeaky-clean body

BUBBLES

BONKERS BUBBLES LOVES to chase bubbles. He has an unending supply rising out of the treasure chest at the bottom of the tank, and he wants every one of those bubbles to be his. When Bubbles meets Nemo, he guards his treasure anxiously. Nemo doesn't mind —after all, he can easily make his own.

Bubbles is a yellow tang fish

Treasure happy
The treasure chest, lying not far from the sunken pirate ship, is one of the more expensive gadgets in the tank, blowing out 100 bubbles per second. Too much time spent in captivity has driven Bubbles mad, and he can think of little else.

Wide mouth

"Bubbles. Bubbles. My bubbles."

Bubble brained
As a tang fish, Bubbles could be related to Dory, which may explain his crazy ideas. Although a keen chaser of bubbles, he has never managed to work out that it's impossible to catch and keep a single one.

Easy target
Bubbles' bright yellow coloring makes him easy to spot in murky waters, which is how he ended up captured and stuck in a tank.

CHUCKLES

A DIME-A-DOZEN goldfish, Chuckles was never one of the most exotic species in the tank, so it was a surprise when Darla picked him out. Unfortunately, Chuckles went belly-up before Darla even took him home, a victim of her shocking habit of shaking the bag to "liven the fish up."

Darla's hand, ever-ready to shake the bag

Photo of fear
Nemo is soon told about the sad fate of Chuckles, and it's a tale not easy to forget—especially as a photo of Darla and her poor pet is clearly visible from the tank.

Poor Chuckles

The porcelain express
Believed to be a goner, Chuckles took the "porcelain express," which means he was flushed down the dentist's toilet and out to sea. But who knows...maybe he was just a good faker, and found his freedom, like Nemo. That's what the Tank Gang hope...

"She wouldn't stop shaking the bag."

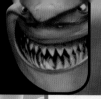

BRUCE

G'DAY MATE! This terrifying eating machine is a reformed character on a caring crusade. Bruce knows that if sharks want to shake off their nasty image, they first have to change themselves. He welcomes all marine life into his vegetarian community, sharing the notion that "fish are friends, not food."

Dangerous den
Bruce's gang think they have found the perfect hang-out—a wreck far from human eyes. But it's actually a sunken submarine, ringed with deadly unexploded mines, and could just be the most dangerous place on the sea bed.

Body built like a torpedo for speed

Sharp teeth of a serious hunter

Party time
When Bruce invites fish to one of his parties, it's hard to say no! In fact, it's hard to say anything when you're petrified with fear.

Food for thought
It's hard to relax around this grinning Great White. Bruce does have the bad habit of calling smaller fish "morsels" and even the tiniest drop of blood in the water sends him into a mad feeding frenzy!

"Fish are friends, not food."

CHUM

CHECK OUT CHUM'S cool face-piercing. This mean-looking mako shark got that souvenir from a run-in with a fisherman who will think twice before angling for sharks again! Rumor has it that Chum is secretly a posh shark who puts on a tough accent to fit in with his gang.

Did You Know?
Chum went to a posh predator boarding school. He worries that his hoity-toity friends will spot him fraternizing with the local reef-raff.

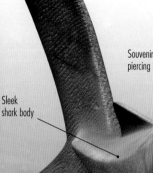

Hero worship
Chum looks up to Bruce and secretly envies his confident public speaking skills.

Diet delight
Marlin and Dory are delighted to hear that Chum and his pals are currently on a fish-free diet.

Souvenir piercing

Sleek shark body

Huge, curved teeth

"We're all mates here, mate."

Happy snacker
Chum can't always control his appetite. When he first meets Marlin and Dory at a meeting, Chum belches up the bony remains of a previous "pal" he brought along. But he is one of the few fish brave enough to intervene when his leader Bruce gets the munchies.

ANCHOR

FOR A HAMMERHEAD, this guy's a softie, and likes nothing better than a group hug. Anchor doesn't always see eye-to-eye with his pals, which isn't surprising considering the shape of his head. He hates being teased about his appearance, so don't mention hammers of any kind in his presence!

Clowning around
Anchor and his mates like nothing better than a good laugh and are excited to have a clown fish at one of their meetings. But Marlin can only fret about his lost son and the gang conclude that he simply isn't very funny.

"Come on, group hug."

Big belly

Did You Know?
Hammerheads have super hearing and can even hear air-bubbles moving through the water!

Chum's chum
Reformed sharks could crack at any moment and turn into savage seafood addicts. It's Anchor's job to keep a close eye on Chum, which is tricky, as his eyes aren't very close to each other.

Fish fads
Anchor likes following fads and loves giving things up. He even tried to give up swimming once, but since sharks have to swim in order to breathe this didn't work out. Anchor's pet hate is dolphins and the way everyone thinks they are cuter than sharks.

NIGEL

HATCHED IN A nest on the roof of the dental surgery, Nigel has fancied himself as an expert on teeth ever since. He likes nothing better than to perch on the windowsill and chat with the Tank Gang about the tricky cases of the day, as long as he doesn't get shooed away by the dentist.

Did You Know?
Nigel has tried to get his pelican pals interested in dentistry, but they just want to sit atop the local bait shop and talk about how stupid seagulls are.

"Hop inside my mouth if you want to live."

Long, thin beak

Feel the pane
Although Dr. P. Sherman is a nature lover, he does draw the line at Nigel treating his dental surgery as a social club. The friendly pelican loses more than a few feathers every week getting the window slammed in his face.

Pelican airways
Nigel's love of gossip comes in handy when he spots Marlin and Dory at the harbor boardwalk. He realizes that these are fish on a mission and fearlessly flies to the rescue.

Nosy Nigel
Nigel is a friendly pelican with a very curious nature—he likes to stick his beak into everything. There's nothing Nigel doesn't know about the goings on around Sydney harbor.

Webbed feet—great for catching crumbs

SQUIRT

FULL OF WONDER and curiosity about the big, bad ocean, Crush's son Squirt is a free spirit just like his dad. But don't be fooled by his cute looks. Squirt is a tough kid who has already survived the ordeal of escaping clawing crabs and hungry seagulls straight after being hatched.

Language barrier
This cool little wave-rider seems to have picked up even more surfing slang than his dad. When he tries to talk to Marlin about cranking cutbacks and screaming bottom curves, the clownfish doesn't understand one word.

"Whoa! That was so cool!"

Jellyman fan
Squirt hero-worships Marlin when he learns of his wild adventures, and thinks he's the bravest fish in the sea. When it's time for the clown fish to leave the East Australian Current, Squirt gives him some advice: rip it, roll it, punch it!

Small back flippers

Squirt's favorite food is seaweed

Devoted dudes
Squirt loves to show his dad his latest stunts. When Crush is really impressed they exchange a flippery high-five, and an affectionate bump of the noggin.

Did You Know
Turtles breathe air using little nostrils near the top of their heads.

CRUSH

CRUISING THE OCEANS in search of the perfect current, Crush is the coolest turtle around. Over many years hanging out on the Australian coast, he has picked up a lot of surfer slang, calling everyone "dude" and thinking that almost everything is truly awesome.

Chillax, dude!
Crush may be the greatest current surfer around, but he insists that Marlin is the one who takes too many risks, and thinks he has serious thrill issues!

"You've got serious thrill issues dude. Awesome."

Dad to dad
These two dads just can't see eye-to-eye on parenting. The laid-back turtle believes in letting his son handle the surf alone and learning to take knocks. Uptight Marlin is naturally horrified.

Streamlined shell to slide through the water

Strong beak for shredding snacks

Strong front flippers to ride the currents

Who's the daddy?
Despite their easy-going, beach-party attitude, turtles are surprisingly tough and can live for many years. Crush considers himself 150 years young, and still shows the little turtles who rules the gnarliest surf out there.

WHALE

LOOKS CAN BE deceiving under the sea, and this "little fella," as Dory calls him on first sight, turns out to be the biggest living creature in the ocean! The beautiful blue whale is grazing on some krill and swallows Marlin and Dory, too. They seem doomed to become his dinner...

Long, thin flippers

Whale talk

Not used to making dinner conversation with its own food, the whale is impressed with Dory's mastery of whale language. She can speak humpback and orca, as well as blue whale.

Pleated grooves expand during feeding

Big mouth swallows up to 40 million krill a day!

Kindly captor

The whale is gigantic, but gentle too. It even gives Marlin and Dory a lift to their destination, and a neat way back to the outside world—through its waterspout. The whale tells Dory when to let go, which is lucky, as letting go is not exactly Marlin's strong suit!

Picking up passengers

With their songs, whales can share news across whole oceans. So maybe this one knew all about Marlin's quest before it took him aboard...

BERNIE AND BAZ

SYDNEY HARBOR IS paradise to greedy crabs, Bernie and Baz. They dine all day on the waste from Sydney's Water Treatment Plant. The crabby crabs guard their grub goldmine jealously and are not very friendly to strange visitors, such as Dory and Nemo.

Back off, Bluey

Bernie and Baz give Dory and Nemo a nasty reception when they come looking for Marlin. But when Dory offers to feed Baz to the local seagulls, the snappy pair agree to help.

"Ah, sweet nectar of life."

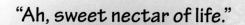

Beady eyes

Bernie

Powerful claws for holding food

Skeleton on outside of body

Shell protects insides

Baz

Did You Know?
Crabs' skeletons are on the outside of their bodies, protecting their internal organs.

Two's company

When Bernie and Baz aren't busy dining, these tough customers are usually shooing nosy neighbors away. They don't want to share their endless buffet with anyone, and pack a mean pincer in self-defense.

DR. SHERMAN

PHILIP SHERMAN uses his dental career to fund his real love—scuba diving. Philip tries to be considerate and only catches fish if he thinks they are struggling for life, which explains why he snaps up poor Nemo, with his weak fin.

"Crikey! All the animals have gone mad!"

Harbor views

P. Sherman often boasts of the views from his surgery. However, it seems the local wildlife prefer the view looking in on him!

Reef raider

Dr. Sherman hits the reef every weekend in his boat, "The Aussie Flosser." A rare find like Nemo is what he lives for.

Fish fanatic

Philip prefers his tank to teeth and even cancels dental appointments in order to clean out his fish tank. All his profits are spent on expensive plastic volcanoes and tiki idol heads to brighten up their lives. If only he knew that all his pets want is to escape!

Sherman would prefer to be wearing a wet suit

DARLA SHERMAN

DR. SHERMAN'S NIECE, Darla, loves fish. She always checks out her uncle's amazing aquarium when she comes for her annual dental appointment, on her birthday. She knows there's usually a gift in that tank for her, and just hopes any new fish will survive a bit longer than the last one did...

"Yeah! Fishy, fishy, fishy!"

Bagging Nemo
It looks like the end for Nemo, when he ends up bagged and at the mercy of Darla—as a very reluctant birthday present. It's as if she sees herself as a piranha, and all other fish as her prey.

Luxury brace set, received at special discount

Birthday bash
The Tank Gang live in fear of Darla's visits to the dentist surgery. On every visit, she terrorizes the poor fish, screaming at them and thumping on the tank to liven them up. She thinks her uncle has very sleepy fish. Maybe the silly gas gets to them, too?

Darla's favorite sweatshirt, a gift from her uncle

Great escape
The fish tormentor finally gets what she deserves when the Tank Gang fights back and helps Nemo to escape.

MR. INCREDIBLE

BOB PARR, aka Mr. Incredible, was once the greatest Super of them all. But then he saved someone who didn't want to be saved, got sued, and was driven into hiding with the rest of his Super family. A normal life beckoned, but Bob is just too big a hero to fit into the everyday world.

Gloved hand

Glory days
Keeping the city safe was all in a day's work for Mr. Incredible back in his superhero glory days. For a while, it seemed he had the world at his feet.

Heroic effort
After years out of action, Bob is more flabby than fit. His biggest battle is just getting into his costume.

Stylish new suit, courtesy of Edna Mode

The Incredibles logo

Did You Know?
As well as being super-strong, Mr. Incredible is fast and agile. His one weakness is a slightly dodgy back.

Back in action
Mr. Incredible is lured out of retirement by a mysterious message offering him the chance to go on a top-secret mission. He is soon on a plane bound for Nomanisan Island and taking on the sinister villain Syndrome. But Bob eventually realizes that his family is really his biggest adventure.

"We're superheroes. What could happen?"

ELASTIGIRL

HELEN PARR, aka Elastigirl, was one of the top Supers on the planet, with the power to stretch her body into any shape imaginable. When Elastigirl met Mr. Incredible, it was love at first sight and together they make an incredible team.

Helen's new suit is virtually indestructible

Doting wife
When she notices that her husband's old costume has been repaired, Helen sets off on a mission to find out why and discovers he is in peril. She packs her new Super suit and flies to Nomanisan Island. Boldly facing any danger, Helen proves that she is still Super.

Super mom
Helen has happily traded the challenges of vanquishing evil for the joys of raising kids. She just wishes Bob would stop living in the past and enjoy the present, too.

Helen is still as Super as she was back in the day

Fire power
When the deadly robot Omnidroid shoots at her son Dash, Helen uses a manhole cover and her stretchy arms to hammer at the robot.

In safe hands
Super-flexible Helen can even stretch herself into a human parachute in an emergency.

"I think you need to be a little more...flexible."

115

VIOLET PARR

A SMART TEENAGER, Violet Parr is a shy girl who yearns for a normal life. She has learnt to hide her feelings behind a sarcastic attitude, and her face behind her long dark hair. It takes a family crisis to make Violet realize just how much she has to offer.

Violet no longer hides behind her hair

Getting noticed
At one time, Violet's crush on Tony Rydinger made her so embarrassed she would disappear rather than face him. But after helping save the world, Violet feels—and looks—different, having finally gained the confidence that she has always lacked.

Shrinking Violet
Violet used to like hiding away in the background of family life. She listened to music and read beauty magazines in her quest to fit in at school and be like everyone else.

"Normal? What *does* anyone in this family know about being normal?"

Feel the force
When danger strikes the family, Violet's true power emerges. In addition to her invisibility, she finds she can create unbreakable spherical force fields.

Practical, stylish thigh-high boots

Visible progress
Now you see her—now you don't! Violet has a tricky time exploiting her powers until brilliant fashion designer Edna Mode creates a special Super suit for her. As Vi's confidence grows, so does her power. She even brushes back her hair and shows the world how incredible she really is.

DASH PARR

DASH IS HIS NAME and speed is his game! Dashiel Parr finds that being the fastest thing on earth, and keeping this cool power a secret, is quite hard to handle when you're only ten years old. Dash has to console himself by playing faster-than-light pranks at school—such as sticking pins on his teacher's chair.

Making a splash
While fleeing Syndrome's minions on Nomanisan Island, Dash makes a cool discovery—he is so fast that he can run right across the water's surface!

Teacher's pest
Being the son of heroes doesn't make you super well-behaved. A frustrated Dash often gets into trouble at school, and a trip back from the Principal's office with mom is not an unusual event for him.

Fast learner
When the family are called into action, Dash finds that he has a lot to learn. Firstly, that all bad guys aren't like the ones on TV shows—they're much scarier—and secondly, that his powers are way cooler than he realized. He even learns to get on with his big sister!

Windswept hair

Cheeky grin

Little legs can run super-fast

"I promise I'll slow up. I'll only be the best by a tiny bit."

JACK-JACK PARR

THE NEWEST MEMBER of the Incredible family, Jack-Jack Parr is seriously cute and his parent's pride and joy. As far as his family knows, Jack-Jack has no super powers—unless it's throwing food, jabbering, and being super cute! But maybe he's just a slow developer...

Monster mode

Turning into a monster is just one of the surprise talents Jack-Jack has been hiding from his parents! He can also defy gravity, pass through walls, and shoot energy beams from his eyes!

Jack-Jack's hair never needs gel

That's my boy

Mr. Incredible is a whole lot happier with family life after getting into hero-action again. Jack-Jack has never had so many super-cuddles.

Even a baby needs to protect his secret identity!

Baby Super

When Syndrome kidnaps Jack-Jack, the teeny tot reveals his awesome transforming powers as a shape-shifter. He turns into living fire, becomes as heavy as lead, and then transforms into a mad mini-fiend. In short, he's too hot to handle.

Baby Super suit

Did You Know?

Jack-Jack's favorite food is mashed carrots and his favorite game is to mash carrots!

FROZONE

LUCIUS BEST, AKA Frozone, was the coolest superhero around. Thanks to his wit and style, and an amazing arsenal of freezing powers, Frozone was one cool customer. Although he seems to have adjusted to civilian life better than his pal Bob, he has kept his Super suit and gadgets.

Did You Know?
The downside of being Frozone is having people make jokes about your power all the time. He has heard Bob's "ice of you to drop by," many times!

"You tell me where my suit is woman! We're talking about the greater good!"

Awesome ally
When the Omnidroid attacks Metroville, Frozone is the only Super who comes to help out the Incredibles. When his ice-handcuffs fail, he freezes up the street, knowing sooner or later the menacing machine will slip up.

Family friend
Lucius is best pals with Mr. Incredible and the whole Parr family adores him. Every Wednesday, Bob and Lucius get together. Their wives think they go bowling—but really they hang out listening to the police radio and reliving their glory days.

Snow motion
Frozone has plenty of cool tricks for getting out of trouble. Ice-skis help him ski-jump to safety.

119

SYNDROME

AFTER MR. INCREDIBLE rejects him as a sidekick, Buddy Pine reinvents himself as the villain Syndrome. An evil genius bent on revenge, Syndrome turns Nomanisan Island into his high-tech hideaway, and terminates every Super he can get his gloves on.

Incrediboy
To start with, Buddy Pine called himself Incrediboy, but he was merely an incredible nuisance. He distracted Mr. Incredible on the disastrous mission that ended with the great hero being sued.

"I'll be a bigger hero than you ever were."

Cape proves to be a fatal mistake for Syndrome

Monologuing maniac
When Syndrome finally captures Mr. Incredible, it is the moment he has spent fifteen years waiting for. However, like all crazy villains, Syndrome is easily tempted into blurting out his evil plans—big mistake.

Hoax hero
Syndrome's master plan is to menace Metroville with his evil Omnidroid, then pretend to defeat it and be hailed as a great new hero. Fortunately, just as he did all those years ago, Mr. Incredible is there to upset Buddy's plans.

Jet boots

MIRAGE

SYNDROME'S accomplice, the alluring and mysterious Mirage, has all the charm and people skills that he lacks. Highly skilled with technology and a master of surveillance, she tracks down the Supers that her boss has targeted, and then lures them into action—for the last time.

Immaculate platinum-blonde hair

Did You Know?
Mirage is so good at spying undercover that, according to the government, she doesn't even officially exist!

"Next time you gamble, bet your own life!"

Secret identity
When Mr. Incredible arrives at Nomanisan Island, Mirage knows how to act as the perfect hostess. She flatters him, pampers his ego, and prepares him for his mission, without once giving away any of her master's real plan.

Slinky satin dress

Changing sides
Mirage confesses that she has a weakness for power. She is loyal to Syndrome until she comes to respect a different kind of strength—the kind that holds the Incredible family together. Mirage knows it's time to change teams.

Life saver
Being held captive, Mr. Incredible has a chance to finish Mirage but he doesn't take it. She is grateful—and impressed by his humanity.

Heels for added height

EDNA MODE

Did You Know?
After Supers were banned, Edna designed clothes for supermodels. But according to E, supermodels are all spoilt, stupid little stick figures!

WORLD-FAMOUS fashion designer Edna "E" Mode is vain, opinionated, and outspoken. She is also brilliant. Her exclusive collections are modeled on catwalks all over the world, but E longs for the days when she created costumes for Supers— and made them look simply fabulous, darling!

Safety first
Edna is obsessed with security. To enter her studio, visitors must pass electric fences, video cameras, and handprint, eyeprint, and voiceprint checks!

Super-slick hair

New challenge
This fast-talking fashion guru can talk anyone into anything. When Bob drops by for a small costume repair, Edna is inspired to re-outfit the whole family— whether they like it or not.

"I never look back darling. It distracts from the now."

Power dressing
Edna is thrilled to design new suits for Bob and his family. Her new range of costumes combine the strength of mega-mesh, with new qualities that imitate the powers of the wearer. Edna does insist on sticking to one rule though—no capes!

Fashion show
Helen is astonished to find that Edna has made new costumes for her family—she had no idea they were still in the hero business!

Edna designs all her own stylish outfits

GILBERT HUPH

THE BOSS OF Insuricare, Gilbert Huph only cares about making a profit, and if that means not paying little old ladies what they're owed, that's fine by Huph. A small-minded man with a pea-sized heart, he is a very big bully in a very little body. Unfortunately, he is also Bob Parr's boss.

Not happy!
Huph has a serious problem with Bob, who actually wants to help people. He summons Bob to his office determined to put a stop to his caring attitude towards customers.

Final straw
Bob blows his cool when halfway through Huph's lecture, Bob sees a man being mugged outside and is unable to help him because Huph threatens to fire him.

Did You Know?
Insuricare has a wide range of customers. Bob usually advises them on how to get around their big bad bureaucracy!

"Tell me how you're keeping Insuricare in the black!"

Huph permanently has the hump

Neatness nut
Gilbert is fixated with order. He likes his pencils neat and tidy and expects his life to be the same. He thinks a company is like an enormous clock, in which all the little cogs have to do their job—make money.

Hospital case
Huph finally pushes Bob too far and gets pushed right back—through several office walls. Gilbert has plenty of time to worry about his own health insurance while lying on a hospital bed.

123

BOMB VOYAGE

AN EXPERT WITH explosives, Bomb Voyage is a stylish super-criminal. He wears the makeup of a French mime artist and conducts all of his in-fight banter in French. Don't be disarmed, however, by his quirky appearance—this eccentric evil-doer is a ruthless fiend, equipped with an ammo belt loaded with deadly bombs.

Familiar foe

Bomb Voyage is an old adversary of Mr. Incredible, and neither are at all surprised to bump into each other during the raid at the Municiberg bank.

"Your outfit is totally ridiculous!"

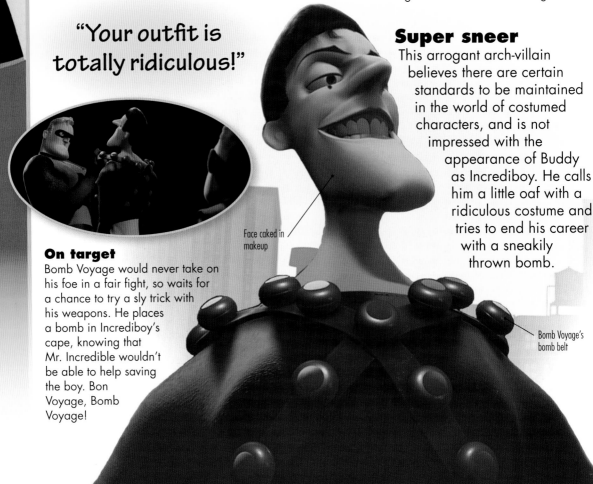

On target

Bomb Voyage would never take on his foe in a fair fight, so waits for a chance to try a sly trick with his weapons. He places a bomb in Incrediboy's cape, knowing that Mr. Incredible wouldn't be able to help saving the boy. Bon Voyage, Bomb Voyage!

Face caked in makeup

Super sneer

This arrogant arch-villain believes there are certain standards to be maintained in the world of costumed characters, and is not impressed with the appearance of Buddy as Incrediboy. He calls him a little oaf with a ridiculous costume and tries to end his career with a sneakily thrown bomb.

Bomb Voyage's bomb belt

OMNIDROID

THIS DIABOLICAL engine of destruction is a learning robot—it studies its opponents, predicts their moves, and exploits their weaknesses. Designed by the fiendish mind of Syndrome, it has been tested on a series of unlucky Supers, and refined until it is smart enough to defeat even Mr. Incredible.

Mean machine
The Omnidroid sounds like every villain's dream weapon. But it has become so smart, that it decides to give the orders rather than take them!

On target
Computer targeting systems lock in on Super foes—and rarely miss.

PLOT ARC   TARGET LOCK

42.000   29.000

NAV 1   NAV2

Enhanced vision for tracking enemies

Master plan
The ultimate destiny of the Omnidroid is to attack Metroville and give its master, Syndrome, the chance to play at saving the world. But Omnidroid has learnt more than Syndrome realizes.

Armored plates

The Omnidroid is built with top-secret metal alloys

Splayed foot-claws allow the Omnidroid to grip any surface

THE UNDERMINER

JUST WHEN THE Incredibles think they have saved Metroville from the forces of evil, up pops another threat to the city. This mole-like monster has come to declare war on peace and happiness—but he has chosen the wrong place to start his career. The Incredibles are on the spot to overpower the Underminer.

To the rescue again
The Parr family shouldn't have put their civilian clothes back on so fast. There's a new bad guy in town and he's out to cause trouble!

"Behold, the Underminer! I'm always beneath you, but nothing is beneath me!"

Tunnel visionary
This diabolical digger wears a miner's helmet with a lamp, so he can see in the dark tunnels he has created beneath the city. No obstacle can block his way, as he travels everywhere in an earth-shaking drilling machine.

Bright light for seei
in dark tunnels

Hard ha

Incredible team
The Incredibles aren't worried about the threat of a new villain in town. There's nothing they love more than a new challenge.

KARI MCKEEN

HELEN PARR WOULD prefer to use a proper babysitting service, but she chooses keen neighbor Kari McKeen to look after Jack-Jack instead. Kari says she has heaps of references and certificates and cannot believe there is anything a baby can dish out that she can't handle. Poor Kari has never looked after a Super baby before...

Brainy baby
Kari is armed with Mozart CDs because she's heard that playing classical music to a baby makes it more intelligent. She wishes her parents had played it to her when she was little—most of the time she doesn't know what other people are talking about!

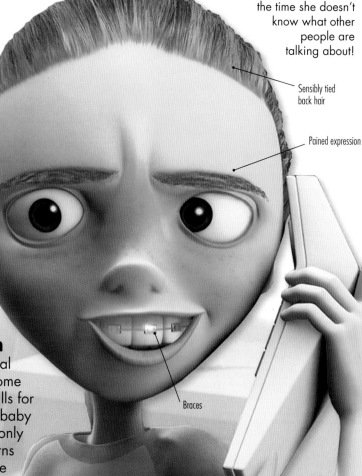

Did You Know?
Kari is so hung up about people spelling her name wrong that she introduces herself as 'Kari with a K and one r and an i.'

Sensibly tied back hair

Pained expression

"Sorry for freakin' out, but your baby has special needs."

Braces

Baby boom
When Jack-Jack starts to reveal his Super powers, Kari is overcome with panic and frantically calls for help. Her opinion is that this baby has special needs and she is only too glad when a relief sitter turns up. It's a shame that it's the sinister supervillain Syndrome...

LIGHTNING MCQUEEN

PISTON CUP LEGEND Lightning McQueen is the greatest race car of his generation. Focused, fierce, and fast, he has an awesome record of results. Although he's a world-famous celebrity, his pals in Radiator Springs ensure his wheels remain firmly on the ground.

Big entrance
Lightning causes mayhem when he accidentally crashes through the sleepy town of Radiator Springs. But all the residents grow to love him—eventually!

Tough competition
Lightning is a champion race car, but he is up against the best of the best from around the globe at the World Grand Prix (WGP). He is hoping that he can maintain his championship record.

"Speed. I am speed."

Star car
Lightning has always found life in the fast lane a real gas—lapping up attention from fans and being treated like a star car. But life at the top can be lonely and Lightning never forgets that his Radiator Springs pals are more important than his career.

Lightning always races in red

Did You Know?
Hotshot race car Lightning has won the Hudson Hornet Memorial Cup once, and the Piston Cup an amazing four times!

State-of-the-art headlights

MATER

RUSTY TOW TRUCK Mater runs Radiator Springs' salvage center. He keeps the residents entertained with his wicked sense of humor and even bigger sense of fun. Loyal Mater is always willing to help his friends and pull them through any crisis.

Disguises and surprises

Agent Mater has a host of disguises and weapons fitted by Agent Holley Shiftwell in a mission to catch the hench car Lemons. They include a rocket-powered jet and computer-generated disguises!

"Wreck? Shoot! I'm the world's best backwards driver!"

Firm friends

Mater's a rusty tow truck and Lightning's a celebrity, but they are still best buddies. When they are both in Radiator Springs, the two are inseparable. Mater usually stays at home when Lightning goes off to race—until the WGP, when Mater becomes part of Team Lightning McQueen!

The fastest tow-rope in Carburetor County!

New adventure

Before meeting Lightning, Mater had never left Radiator Springs. However, a case of mistaken identity at the WGP sees Mater thrust into a secret mission with the British Intelligence. Pretty soon, Mater proves he is one brave tow truck.

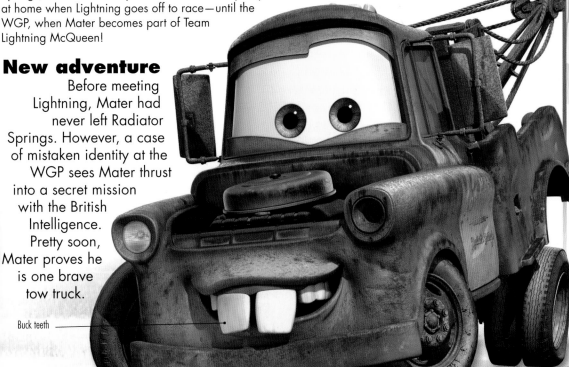

Buck teeth

DOC HUDSON

Did You Know?
Doc Hudson's licence plate reads 51HHMD, a reference to his year and track number (51 model (Hudson Hornet), and profession (Medical Doctor).

DOC HUDSON IS ONE of the most respected residents of Radiator Springs. As the town's motor-medic, he gives the citizens thorough checkups at his medical clinic. He is also the town judge. Sadly, Doc is no longer with us, but his spirit lives on in Radiator Springs.

Doc's orders
Doc challenges Lightning to a race at Willy's Butte to teach the arrogant youngster a thing or two. Sure enough, the wise Doc wins and Lightning ends up in a bed of cacti!

Back on track
Doc goes back to the racetrack to support his new pal Lightning as his crew chief. With a Fabulous Hudson Hornet paint job from Ramone, the racing legend wins a round of applause from the crowd.

"Was that floating like a Cadillac, or was that stinging like a beemer?"

Hidden Hudson
Doc Hudson has a secret under his hood! He's actually the legendary Fabulous Hudson Hornet, the three times winner of the Piston Cup from 1951 to 1953. But his career ended abruptly when he crashed, and everyone seemed more interested in new cars.

Shiny chrome

SALLY

BRILLIANT AND BEAUTIFUL, sleek Sally runs the *Cozy Cone* motel in Radiator Springs. She used to live life in the fast lane as a lawyer until she discovered Radiator Springs and fell in love with the town and its residents. The plucky Porsche is determined to do all she can to put her beloved town back on the map.

Did You Know?

Sally sports a small, pinstripe tattoo on her rear. When Lightning notices it, Sally is very embarrassed!

Road to romance

When Sally meets Lightning, she is not impressed by his smart one-liners or the revving of his engine. Later, on a long drive through Carburetor County, Sally discovers a kinder, more open-hearted Lightning.

Legal whiz

Sally still uses her legal training as the town's attorney. She has a strong sense of justice and is very confident in court.

"Do you want to stay at the *Cozy Cone* or what?"

Grand plans

Sally is a car with big dreams and grand schemes. She plans to reopen the legendary *Wheel Well* Hotel on Route 66, which will really help get the forgotten town back on the map.

Lightweight alloy wheels

GUIDO

COMPACT ITALIAN forklift Guido is the fastest tire changer in town, and probably the world! He works with his best pal Luigi at *Casa Della Tires*. The tiny forklift has a big dream—to change the tires on a real race car, preferably a Ferrari!

Proud pitty
At the Piston Cup, Guido does Radiator Springs (and Italy) proud. During the tie-breaker race, he performs a pit stop on Lightning so quick that his movements are a blur.

Luigi is happiest when he's changing tires

"Pit stop!"

True colors
At Willy's Butte, Guido shows his support for Lightning—by waving a Ferrari flag!

Fastest forklift around

Dream come true
The fanatical forklift's ultimate dream to be a pitty is realized twice—first at the Piston Cup and again at the WGP. At both races, nimble Guido shrugs off the doubts of the other pit crews and really shows them how it's done!

LUGI

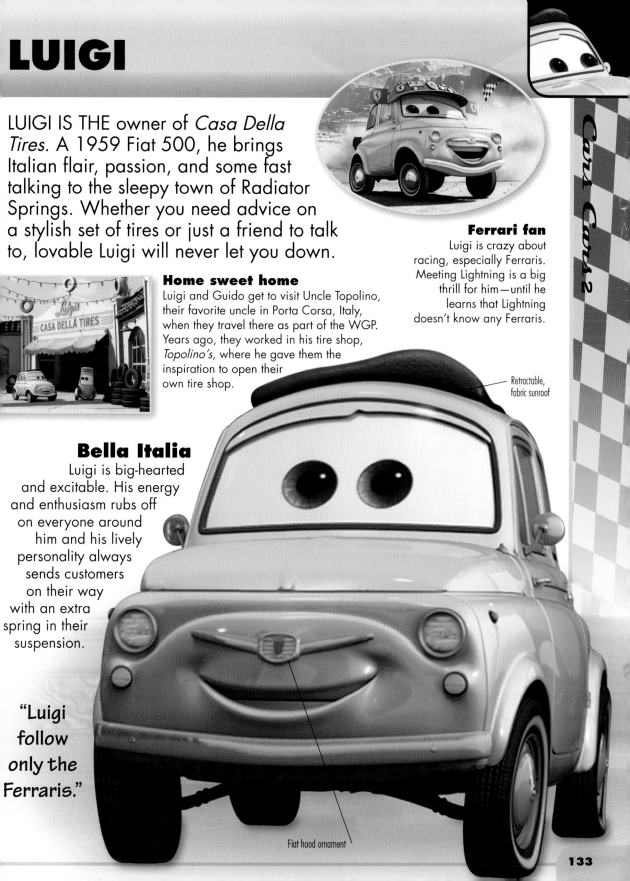

LUIGI IS THE owner of *Casa Della Tires*. A 1959 Fiat 500, he brings Italian flair, passion, and some fast talking to the sleepy town of Radiator Springs. Whether you need advice on a stylish set of tires or just a friend to talk to, lovable Luigi will never let you down.

Ferrari fan
Luigi is crazy about racing, especially Ferraris. Meeting Lightning is a big thrill for him—until he learns that Lightning doesn't know any Ferraris.

Home sweet home
Luigi and Guido get to visit Uncle Topolino, their favorite uncle in Porta Corsa, Italy, when they travel there as part of the WGP. Years ago, they worked in his tire shop, *Topolino's*, where he gave them the inspiration to open their own tire shop.

Bella Italia
Luigi is big-hearted and excitable. His energy and enthusiasm rubs off on everyone around him and his lively personality always sends customers on their way with an extra spring in their suspension.

"Luigi follow only the Ferraris."

Retractable, fabric sunroof

Fiat hood ornament

RAMONE

RAMONE IS A 1959 Chevrolet and the coolest car in Radiator Springs. He runs his *House of Body Art*, Radiator Springs' custom paint shop, and makes sure he gives himself a new coat of paint several times a week. Ramone is often seen out cruising with his wife, Flo.

Cars Cars 2

Cool customer
Before Lightning sets off to show the world what he's made of at the WGP, he stops off at Ramone's to get a brand new paint job. Ramone works his magic and Lightning looks brand new!

Arty car
Ramone is an artist with an airbrush and a magician with paint and metal. Whether you want a flame job, ghost flames, or even some old-school pinstripes "Von Dutch" style, Ramone will paint you right up.

True romance
Ramone and Flo's relationship is as strong as the day they first met and they have become Radiator Springs' premier couple!

Flashy flame paint job

Hydraulics allow Ramone to ride high or low

"Oh, yeah, baby!"

134

FLO

FLO IS A CLASSIC show car from the 1950s. Sassy and sleek, she has been running *Flo's V8 Café* for years. Everyone knows the town would fall apart without Flo—there would be no one to sell gasoline and oil, or dish out sage advice.

Heart and soul
Cars are guaranteed a warm welcome at *Flo's V8 Café*. The town's residents gather there every day to sip oil and catch up on local gossip.

Come on in
Friendly Flo is always on the lookout for new customers to dazzle with her unique brand of Carburetor County hospitality.

"I have gas! Lots of gas!"

Flo's show
As a show car, Flo used to travel across the country, modeling her beautiful curves and swooping fins. When she passed through Radiator Springs, she fell in love with Ramone, and never left the little town.

Flo is always spotless

Super-sleek curves

Knock-out smile

135

SHERIFF

STRAIGHT-TALKING, hardworking, and honest, Sheriff is driven by a strong sense of duty—protecting the good citizens of Radiator Springs. He takes the job very seriously: Any troublemakers will be taken straight to Traffic Court, and Sheriff may even siphon off their gas so they can't escape!

Nap time

Radiator Springs is a sleepy town where lawbreaking is rare. This means that Sheriff can often be found taking a nap at his favorite spot behind the billboard.

Take a break

Sheriff loves to drop in at *Flo's V8 Café* for a quart of oil and to tell stories about his days on the old Highway 66.

> "I haven't gone this fast in years. I'm gonna blow a gasket or somethin'."

Worn out cop

Sheriff is not in tip-top condition. Pursuing Lightning McQueen at high speeds leaves the law enforcer exhausted; in fact he backfires so many times, Lightning thinks he's being shot at! Perhaps Sheriff has just enjoyed too much oil at *Flo's V8 Café*.

Siren ensures the Sheriff is heard before he is seen

Gotcha!

When Lightning McQueen breaks the speed limit, Sheriff is already waiting on the edge of town to try and catch him!

Tendency to backfire at high speeds

RED

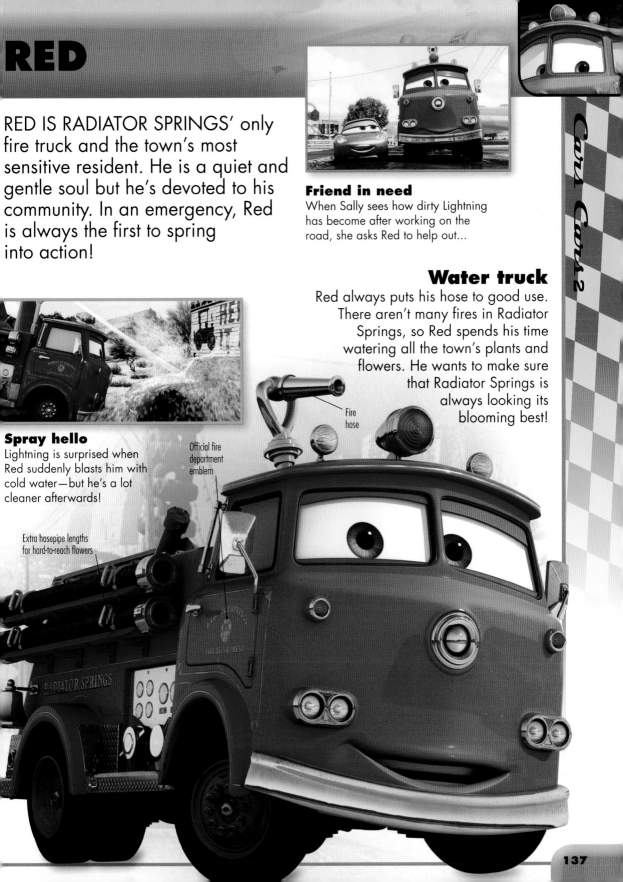

RED IS RADIATOR SPRINGS' only fire truck and the town's most sensitive resident. He is a quiet and gentle soul but he's devoted to his community. In an emergency, Red is always the first to spring into action!

Friend in need
When Sally sees how dirty Lightning has become after working on the road, she asks Red to help out...

Water truck
Red always puts his hose to good use. There aren't many fires in Radiator Springs, so Red spends his time watering all the town's plants and flowers. He wants to make sure that Radiator Springs is always looking its blooming best!

Spray hello
Lightning is surprised when Red suddenly blasts him with cold water—but he's a lot cleaner afterwards!

Extra hosepipe lengths for hard-to-reach flowers

Fire hose

Official fire department emblem

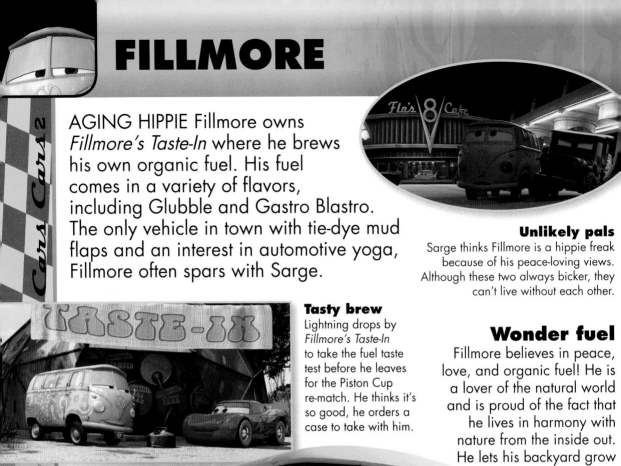

FILLMORE

AGING HIPPIE Fillmore owns *Fillmore's Taste-In* where he brews his own organic fuel. His fuel comes in a variety of flavors, including Glubble and Gastro Blastro. The only vehicle in town with tie-dye mud flaps and an interest in automotive yoga, Fillmore often spars with Sarge.

Cars Cars 2

Unlikely pals
Sarge thinks Fillmore is a hippie freak because of his peace-loving views. Although these two always bicker, they can't live without each other.

Tasty brew
Lightning drops by *Fillmore's Taste-In* to take the fuel taste test before he leaves for the Piston Cup re-match. He thinks it's so good, he orders a case to take with him.

Wonder fuel
Fillmore believes in peace, love, and organic fuel! He is a lover of the natural world and is proud of the fact that he lives in harmony with nature from the inside out. He lets his backyard grow "naturally," always recycles, and only uses his own organic fuel.

Environmental stickers

Laid-back expression

Paintings are Fillmore's own designs

CARBURETOR
51237
COUNTY

SARGE

EX-ARMY JEEP Sarge brings military discipline to Radiator Springs. He runs *Sarge's Surplus Hut*, which is polished to a shiny sheen and fronted by a super-neat lawn. Sarge has traditional views and disagrees with hippie cars like Fillmore. However, his bark is worse than his bite and he can always be relied on to help his pals.

Opposites attract

Sarge lives next door to Fillmore. His tidy hut and garden is the complete opposite to Fillmore's free-flowin' backyard.

Attention!

Sarge brings a sense of duty and military discipline to Team Lightning McQueen at the WGP—when he's not bickering with Fillmore, that is.

"Oh, take a carwash, hippie."

Military mind

Being from a military background, Sarge follows a highly disciplined routine. Each morning the patriotic soldier raises the Stars and Stripes and salutes it with his antenna. However, Fillmore's less keen on being woken up by the trumpets of "Reveille"!

Did You Know?

Sarge served in the military, where he received the Grille Badge of True Mettle for his bravery.

LIZZIE

LIZZIE IS Radiator Springs' most senior citizen. Nevertheless, she's got more gumption than cars half her age. With her mischievous sense of humor, occasional outspoken comments, and unreliable memory, many townsfolk think she's slightly bonkers!

Legend
Lizzie was married to Stanley, who founded Radiator Springs in 1909. He is immortalized as a statue outside the fire station and Lizzie visits it every day, remembering the good times they had together.

Lizzie's Wares
Lizzie owns a curio shop, and she can often be found taking a well-earned nap outside. The shop sells everything from Route 66 memorabilia to souvenir snow globes.

"You keep talking to yourself, people will think you're crazy!"

Did You Know?
Lizzie first drove into Radiator Springs in 1927. Although Stanley had to ask Lizzie out a few times before she actually said yes, the pair soon became inseparable.

Plain speaker
Lizzie believes in always telling it like it is, no matter what others may think (even if she can't remember exactly what "it" is!) Her straight-talking comments often surprise the younger inhabitants of Radiator Springs.

Squeaky parts need plenty of oil

FRANK AND THE TRACTORS

THE FIELDS AROUND Radiator Springs are full of tractors, happily grazing, munching, and chewing. These creatures aren't clever—they eat and sleep, and then eat and sleep a bit more. The tractors are supervised by Frank—a combine harvester and ten tons of angry agricultural machinery.

Tractor tipping

Tractors are dozy, docile, and dopey. They are the perfect targets for Mater's favorite pastime—tractor tipping. One honk from the cheeky tow truck and the tractors are so startled, they tip over backward!

Mud splotches

CHEWALL

Arghhhhh!

Mater takes Lightning for some tractor tipping late one night, but fun turns to fear when Frank appears on the scene. As he comes after Mater and Lightning, they do what any car would do—flee!

Fierce Frank

Frank the Combine doesn't take kindly to anyone messing with his tractors. If anyone upsets him or his tractors, ferocious Frank will chase after them. When his rotating blades are bearing down on you, it's probably time to make a run for it.

Beware of Frank's rotating blades!

THE KING

STRIP "THE KING" Weathers is racing royalty. Not only has he won seven Piston Cups but he has also won over virtually everyone he's met. This track legend is the perfect professional—a true gent and good sport on and off the track. He's just a regular guy who regularly wins everything!

Pushing in
In The King's final race of his final season, he crashes yards from the finishing line, after being slammed by Chick Hicks. Lightning honorably pushes The King to the finish line, so the respected race car can bow out on a high.

Lovely Lynda
The King's wife, Lynda, is the veteran race car's #1 fan. Win or lose, The King is always her champion.

"You ain't gonna win unless you've got good folks behind you..."

Team player
The King wouldn't have won seven Piston Cups without having a fabulous team around him. From his Dinoco sponsors to his pit crew, they offer The King the loyalty, friendship, and darn fast pit stops he values above all else.

Rear spoiler keeps The King firmly on the racetrack at high speeds

Dinoco logo—the mark of a champion!

Dinoco Blue paint job

CHICK HICKS

ROTTEN RACER Chick Hicks is desperate to win a Piston Cup. He has bumped and cheated his way to more second places than any car in history, always finishing as runner-up to The King. With The King about to retire, Chick is sure this is his chance to be a winner.

Mean green team
Chick's team is the pits. They laugh at Chick's terrible jokes and wear equally terrible mustaches.

Did You Know?
Lightning gives Chick a nickname—"Thunder"—because thunder always comes after lightning!

Hollow victory
Chick finally wins the Piston Cup, but nobody cheers. Everyone has witnessed his dirty tricks and bad sportsmanship and they boo him off the podium.

Chick the chump
Chick Hicks's biggest fan is himself. He believes he is talented, handsome, and hilarious. However, only his team and pit crew agree— and that's because he pays them to!

"The Piston Cup—it's mine, dude, it's mine!"

High-visibility advertising space

Beady eyes

Clip-on mustache

Chick's official sponsor: Hostile Takeover Bank

RUSTY AND DUSTY

BROTHERS RUSTY AND Dusty Rust-eze are the joint founders of Rust-eze Medicated Bumper Ointment. They sponsor Lightning McQueen, but he thinks the shabby duo are bad for his hotshot image, despite the fact that they gave him his first big break.

Promotion
Rusty and Dusty host the Rust-eze hospitality tent at races to promote their Medicated Bumper Ointment.

Rusty is literally falling apart

Rust and corrosion on body

Rusty
Rusty is a 1963 Dodge Dart vehicle. He finds even the slightest thing incredibly funny, and so does his brother.

A squirt of Rust-eze is needed!

Large windscreen

Dusty's windows are dusty

Dusty
Dusty is a 1967 Dodge Van. Not content with laughing at his own worn-out jokes, he also enjoys poking fun at Lightning, particularly his car sticker headlights.

"We might even clear enough to buy you some headlights!"

Headlights barely emit light because they are so dusty

Cars

MIA AND TIA

IDENTICAL TWINS MIA and Tia are Lightning McQueen's biggest fans. The glamorous groupies cheer him on whenever and wherever they can. The only way to tell these two sisters apart is by their license plates.

Super fans
Mia and Tia go to all of Lightning's races. When he flashes his lucky lightning bolt, they practically faint with excitement!

Retractable hood

Red paint job to match Lightning's

Mia
Mia and her sister Tia are covered in stickers in honor of their hero Lightning. Replica lightning bolts, Lightning's race number 95, and, of course, some heart stickers all show that they are his #1 fans.

The twins are adorned with love heart stickers

Tia is often in awe of Lightning's skills on the race track

"We love you, Lightning!"

Tia
Mia and Tia prove to be fickle fans. When Lightning goes missing before the final race of the Piston Cup, they switch their allegiance to his rival Chick Hicks!

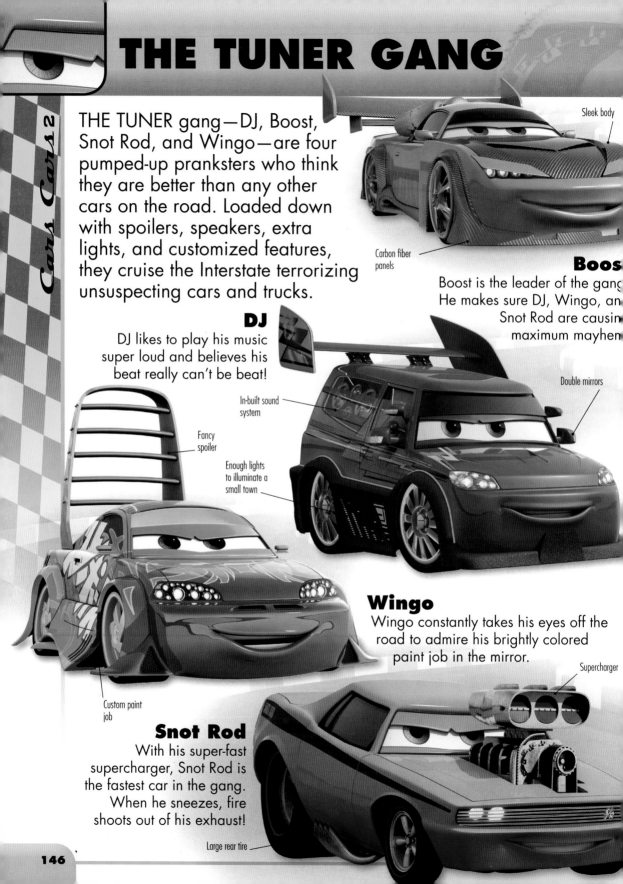

THE TUNER GANG

THE TUNER gang—DJ, Boost, Snot Rod, and Wingo—are four pumped-up pranksters who think they are better than any other cars on the road. Loaded down with spoilers, speakers, extra lights, and customized features, they cruise the Interstate terrorizing unsuspecting cars and trucks.

Sleek body

Carbon fiber panels

Boos

Boost is the leader of the gang He makes sure DJ, Wingo, an Snot Rod are causin maximum mayhen

DJ

DJ likes to play his music super loud and believes his beat really can't be beat!

In-built sound system

Fancy spoiler

Enough lights to illuminate a small town

Double mirrors

Wingo

Wingo constantly takes his eyes off the road to admire his brightly colored paint job in the mirror.

Supercharger

Custom paint job

Snot Rod

With his super-fast supercharger, Snot Rod is the fastest car in the gang. When he sneezes, fire shoots out of his exhaust!

Large rear tire

TEX

TEX IS A SMOOTH-TALKING Texan and the owner of the mighty oil company, Dinoco. He is honest, honorable, and, above all, loyal. Tex holds the keys to the hottest sponsorship deal in racing—every car would love to be a Dinoco race car. He is on the lookout for a successor to The King, who is due to retire.

Good guy
Nice guy Tex is extremely generous. He even lets Lightning's new pal Mater take a ride in his luxury executive helicopter!

Dream sponsor
Tex is used to race cars schmoozing him to try and get the sponsorship that all race cars dream of. The accompanying fame, money, and glamorous lifestyle certainly fire up Chick's engine!

Did You Know?
Dinoco's success is down to a hard-working and harmonious team. The King and Tex are great friends, and have been together for years.

"You sure made Dinoco proud. Thank you King."

Dedicated
Tex knows it takes a lot of hard work and dedication to win—he started Dinoco with just one small oil well and it's now the largest oil company in the world! He values loyalty and fair play above instant success.

Metallic gold paint job

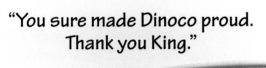

FINN MCMISSILE

FINN MCMISSILE is a suave secret agent from British Intelligence. Cool, cunning, and charismatic, Finn remains unflappable even in extreme danger. Slick spy skills, plus a stockpile of gadgets mean that Finn can maneuver his way out of the tightest corners and stickiest situations.

Sly spy
Finn is an expert at hiding in the shadows. When he uncovers a plot by Professor Z to disrupt the World Grand Prix, Finn gets ready for the mission of a lifetime.

"I haven't properly introduced myself. Finn McMissile, British Intelligence."

On fire
Finn's rocket launchers are concealed in his headlights. When this secret agent sets his sight on a target, he never misses.

Tails cut through currents

Gadgets galore
Finn's cool collection of gadgets includes rocket launchers, a secret camera, and a glass-cutting machine. They are cunningly concealed to make sure enemy agents are taken by surprise!

Tires extend out for extra flotation

Finn's fins

HOLLEY SHIFTWELL

BRITISH AGENT Holley Shiftwell is fresh out of the secret agent academy. She knows the training manual by heart but has not yet experienced a real mission. When she unexpectedly finds herself working in the field with Finn McMissile, the brave agent shifts up a gear and prepares to face real danger for the first time!

Under pressure

Holley feels under pressure working with top secret agent Finn McMissile. However, she is a hard worker and a fast learner and is sure she can impress the experienced agent with her enthusiasm.

Rear tail extends upward when in flight mode

Secret wings unfold out of side

Holley has a stash of hidden gadgets to surprise the enemy

Gadget geek

High-tech Holley is fitted out with all the latest gadgets and gizmos. She's never used them in the field though, and she can't wait to test them on her first mission.

Rookie no more

Finn has never worked with an agent who has so much high-tech equipment under her hood. But Holley shows him that her gadgets, such as her onboard computer, are invaluable when hunting down the enemy!

SIDDELEY

SIDDELEY IS A slick British secret service jet plane. He spends his time flying other agents on top-secret missions and then dropping them right in the danger zone. Silver-bodied Siddeley is ultra-reliable and incredibly brave, and agents breathe sighs of relief when he swoops in to rescue them!

On approach!
Siddeley comes to Finn and Mater's rescue when they are being attacked by the Lemons. He then flies them and Holley Shiftwell from Tokyo to Paris.

Twin jet engines

Sleek body aerodynamically designed to reach super-fast speeds

Did You Know?
One of Siddeley's close pals is Stephenson, a spy train that takes Finn, Holley, and Mater from Paris to Italy.

Techno jet
Siddeley is packed full of the latest state-of-the-art gadgets. With his ultra-powerful twin engine, radar-beating cloaking technology, and arsenal of high-tech weapons, he's fine-tuned for the highest performance!

"I'm on approach!"

Come fly with me
Siddeley and Finn McMissile have completed many missions together. Finn trusts Siddeley to always fly to his rescue.

ROD "TORQUE" REDLINE

ROD "TORQUE" REDLINE is an American secret agent and one of the finest in the force. As a muscle car, he has extra strength. However, he is also able to flex other powers, including intelligence, quick wits, and the ability to completely change his appearance!

Mission possible
Rod has vital information regarding the plot to sabotage the WGP. He has to pass it on to another agent and nothing, not even a mean Lemon, is going to get in his way!

High pressure
With the bad guys hot on his tail, Rod has no choice but to pass the information to rusty truck Mater. What's the worse that could happen?

Cool customer
Redline is renowned for his ability to stay calm under pressure. Worrying is for wimps and can compromise a mission! Even near his untimely end, when Professor Z threatens him with his secret weapon, Redline continues to insult the Lemons!

His expression hides a calm manner

Did You Know?
Rod is a master of disguises. He is even able to disguise himself as a Lemon car!

Concealed gun

FRANCESCO BERNOULLI

ITALIAN GRAND PRIX champion Francesco Bernoulli is Lightning McQueen's major rival to win the World Grand Prix. Fast, flash, and a total show-off, he is the most successful race car in Europe. But despite Bernoulli's big-mouth bravado, he really respects his rivals and is a good sport.

Attention seeker

Francesco enjoys nothing more than being in the spotlight. When the attention isn't on him, a spin on one of his sleek, 100% Italian Rotelli tires is sure to get the press bulbs flashing again.

"Francesco is TRIPLE speed!"

Numero uno

Francesco uses sheer power to get ahead of his rivals on the track. But he also has some special tactics to rile his rivals, like teasing.

Francesco's fans

Francesco has a huge following of fans from around the world. They admire his sleek finish and open wheels. The Italian fans love to get behind their hero, particularly when he races at his hometown track of Porta Corsa!

Did You Know?

When Francesco was young, he would sneak into the famous Monza racecourse and practice for hours.

Red, white, and green paint job — the colors of the Italian flag

Francesco is streamlined to perfection

CARLA VELOSO

CARLA VELOSO IS flying the flag for girl racers everywhere—she is the only female competing in the World Grand Prix. From Rio De Janeiro, Brazil, the South American superstar car loves to samba. Her sense of rhythm and car-nival spirit help give her both amazing power and superb stamina.

Determined rookie
The World Grand Prix is Carla's first major race. She is determined to put Brazil on the racing map!

Did You Know?
Carla's race number is 8. She set a new track record on her local circuit.

Sight-seeing
Carla feels at home cruising around Japan's streets. They remind her of her home country, Brazil, because of the bright lights and bustling crowds.

Carla's crisis
When Veloso comes third in the Tokyo WGP race, she's on top form. However, in Italy she's hit by Professor Z's secret weapon and her fuel tank explodes. With the London race looming, this puts Carla in a fix. Luckily, she is fully repaired and ready to race in time!

World Grand Prix deco

Detailed design inspired by Car-nival in Brazil

Electric blue hubcaps

SHU TODOROKI

SHU TODOROKI IS A LMP-type race car from Japan. His red and white paint job and Japanese dragon design reflect his proud Japanese heritage. Shu is focused, fierce, and flies along at enormous speeds. He grew up at the base of an active volcano, which perhaps explains his fiery personality!

Did You Know?
Shu is a Le Mans Prototype race car. This means that he is custom-built for sports car and endurance racing.

Seven setback

Shu is targeted by the Lemons at the Porta Corsa race and his engine explodes! But despite this setback, strong Shu recovers and makes it to the final race in London.

Winning team

Shu's crew chief, Mach Matsuo, is the only Japanese race car ever to win at Le Mans—a tough 24-hour race in France. So Shu knows he is on the right track to success.

On target

Shu is the Suzaka Champion of Japan, making him a fierce contender at the World Grand Prix. He hopes to prove his champion-level skills and do his home country proud.

Lightweight wing mirror

Legendary red dragon deco

JEFF GORVETTE

JEFF GORVETTE IS an all-American racing hero. His consistent top ten finishes led to him being crowned Rookie of the Year and means he is a strong entrant into the World Grand Prix. With the Stars and Stripes incorporated into his paint job, this rising star has already earned his stripes!

Stocky build
Jeff Gorvette might not be as streamlined as the other WGP contenders, but his strong body and legendary endurance make him a lethal opponent.

"Can you believe this party?"

Legends
Jeff is well known in the racing world for his awesome accelerating abilities. He is supported by his crew chief, John Lassetire, who is known for his decisive leadership and ability to get the job done.

Grand Gorvette
Jeff Gorvette is a Grand Touring car and always appears as number 24. He's so dedicated to his sport, he moved to Indiana to be nearer to the racing action. The move pays off—Gorvette manages to complete all three WGP races, keeping his incredible record intact.

Stars and Stripes of American flag

Jeff is on a mission to win the WGP!

MILES AXLEROD

MILES AXLEROD is a filthy rich oil tycoon. However, he appears to have decided to use his powers (and trunkful of money) to make the world a better place. An environmental campaigner, Miles has converted to electricity and is promoting Allinol, a cheap and safe eco-friendly fuel.

Electric dreams
Axlerod used to be a gas guzzler, but now he is customized to within an inch of his life to be environmentally friendly. The wire coils in his wheels are connected to an electric battery and he even has a solar panel on his roof!

New fuel
Miles creates the World Grand Prix to demonstrate the power of Allinol. All the race cars, including Lightning McQueen, are using it.

"Alternative energy is the future!"

Greedy not green
Actually, the only green thing about Miles Axlerod is his paint job. The tycoon is more evil than eco-friendly and is behind an elaborate plot to destroy race cars and discredit Allinol forever, so he can get rich from oil again!

Allinol logo is on grille

Green paint job to match green views

Wire coils in wheels are connected to electric battery

PROFESSOR Z

PROFESSOR Z IS A mad scientist with a twisted mind. The monocle-wearing inventor spends his time designing dangerous weapons and hatching dastardly plots. His latest venture is a plot to disrupt the WGP and turn the world against alternative energy, so that cars will rely on gasoline and bring profits to the Lemon cars.

Wicked weapon
Professor Z's deadly electromagnetic radiation ray is disguised as a camera. It might just be the Professor's most brilliant invention yet. However, the mad scientist isn't counting on a rusty tow truck foiling his plan!

First to go
Secret agent Rod "Torque" Redline is the Professor's first victim. The tough agent doesn't stand a chance against his deadly invention.

"Now no one can stop us!"

A monocle is the trademark of evil geniuses everywhere

Evil minions
Professor Z doesn't work alone—he controls a large and loyal army of very bitter Lemons. They are keen to carry out orders for the unhinged Professor, lured by the promise of the spare parts they crave.

The rusty Professor could use a spray of Rust-eze!

Z 750

157

Cars 2

UNCLE AND MAMA Topolino are Luigi's favorite uncle and aunt. They live in the pretty Italian village of Santa Routina, near Porto Corsa. Uncle Topolino inspired Luigi and Guido to open their own tire shop, *Casa Della Tires*, in Radiator Springs!

Welcome!

The Topolinos are full of warmth and wisdom. They prove that Italian hospitality can't be topped when they invite Lightning's entire pit crew to stay.

Soft top is still in great condition

Wise guy

Uncle Topolino is the oldest car in town, but with years of experience under his hood, he's also the wisest! Cars travel for miles to visit Topolino's village tire shop, to ask advice on everything from tires to friendship.

"A wise car hears one word and understands two."

Fiat tires

Creamy paint job

Elegant whitewall tires

Full on fuel

Mama Topolino believes the secret to a happy car is a full stomach. She produces the finest fuel in Santa Routina and has made it her mission to make sure the villagers are well fed with her homemade recipe.

VICTOR H

THE LEMON FAMILIES are controlled by powerful Lemonheads. Victor H is head of the Hugo Lemon family. He is in serious need of repair and is known to break down often. But Victor's not worried—he's got a personal chauffeur, Ivan, to tow him around!

"Is the Big Boss here yet?"

The help
Tough truck Ivan is not only Victor's chauffeur, he is also his personal bodyguard. However, Ivan is easily distracted, especially if the distraction is a pretty sports cars with a flat tire.

V for victory
Victor is a very rich villain. He has made huge amounts of money running a network of corrupt oil refineries. Now that he has worked himself up to the position of Head of the Hugos, he intends to run the crime organization like the well-oiled machine that he's not.

Aggressive expression

Did You Know?
The Lemons are divided into four families, namely the Hugos, Gremlins, Pacers, and Trunkovs.

Victor leaks little and often

159

TOMBER

TINY TOMBER IS a French three-wheeler-dealer. He has a market stall where he sells old spare parts from a variety of sources, but the dubious dealer never reveals where he got them all from. Tomber's name means "to fall" in French. This three-wheeler is sometimes a little unsteady!

Foreign friends
Mater and Tomber hit it off straight away. They have mutual respect for each other because of their extensive knowledge of car engines and parts.

Tomber the trader
Tomber is actually one of Finn McMissile's secret informants. The wobbly three-wheeler feeds Finn with information on the Lemons and their attempts to get special spare parts.

In the know
Tomber and Finn have worked together for many years. There's nothing this tiny car doesn't know about cars!

Deep concentration

Mirror close to eyes

Two lights to see small spare parts

Unstable wheel

"Are you kidding me?"

GREM AND ACER

GREM AND ACER are Professor Z's chief henchcars. They are both Lemons—members of a global gang of cars with design faults and performance issues. Made bitter by their problems, the Lemons join Professor Z in his scheme to become the most powerful cars in the world.

Lemon head
Acer isn't afraid to do Professor Z's dirty work. Via a headset, he obediently takes orders to blow up the WGP race cars as they speed past.

"Smile for the camera!"

Acer could use a new paint job

Acer
Rusty and dented, Acer the Pacer has always felt like an outcast in the car world. He isn't afraid to get his wheels dirty by doing Professor Z's evil bidding.

Bumper could fall off at any moment

Grem is in serious need of a wash

Grem
Grim Grem is envious of any cars that are polished, sleek, and with all their parts intact. The only positive thing about Grem is that he enjoys his work!

Grim, determined expression

REMY

RATATOUILLE

RATS AREN'T supposed to like humans, and they certainly aren't supposed to have a passion for cooking. But Remy isn't like other rats, who spend their time eating trash, dodging traps, and avoiding poison. Remy has a special talent and he dreams of being a famous chef, just like his hero Auguste Gusteau.

Nosing around

Remy has a highly developed sense of smell and taste. These skills help to make him a great chef, but they are also pretty useful skills for a rat. Remy is the best poison-checker in the whole colony.

> "If you are what you eat, then I only want to eat the good stuff."

Anyone can cook

When the food critic Anton Ego demands dinner, Remy knows just what to make—ratatouille. After a single bite, the famous critic is a changed man and declares that Remy is "the finest chef in France."

Sensitive nose

Lucky break

Remy's curiosity about humans leads to trouble, just as his Dad said it would. The rat colony has to flee its home, thanks to Remy, while he ends up alone in Paris. Fortunately, he finds himself right outside Gusteau's restaurant.

Hygienically clean paws

Natural chef

At first, Remy's pal Linguini gets all the credit for being the exciting new chef. When the truth is revealed, it takes a while for everyone to get used to the idea, but with a pinch of luck, a dollop of friendship, and a *soupçon* of talent, Remy finally finds the recipe for success.

LINGUINI

Did You Know?

Linguini has been fired from every job he has ever had. Working at *Gusteau's* is his last chance.

WHEN CLUMSY garbage boy Linguini spills the soup in *Gusteau's* kitchen, it turns out to be the luckiest accident he has ever had. Remy saves the soup, and Linguini's job, and the unlikely pair form a double act that will change both of their lives.

In control

Linguini has a problem: He can't actually cook, but Remy can. Clever Remy has an idea—he hides under Linguini's chef's hat and guides his movements by pulling his hair. Amazingly, it works!

Ill-fitting chef's uniform

Food of love

It's not always fun being controlled by a rat, but Linguini finds some unexpected benefits. Not only does the "little chef" take control in the kitchen, he also gives his shy pal a head start with his love life.

"You know how to cook and I know how to appear human."

An heir in the soup

Linguini is Auguste Gusteau's secret son, but he has none of his father's talent. However, when Remy's soup is a hit, Linguini gets the credit and is asked to make it all over again. With Remy's help, Linguini is a success.

True chums

Taking a chance on a talented rat is the smartest thing Linguini has ever done. His life has never been better!

Beat-up old sneakers

SKINNER

SNEAKY CHEF Skinner is a small guy with big plans. After chef Gusteau's death, he becomes Head Chef and doesn't let anyone forget who's boss. The short-tempered chef rules the kitchen by fear. However, when he meets an even smaller chef, Skinner finally gets what he deserves.

Large toque (chef's hat)

Ratting them out

Linguini and Remy are too smart for Skinner, but the mean chef has the last laugh. He reports the rat infestation to the health inspector and *Gusteau's* is closed down!

"You're fired!"

Mean expression

Short-term thinking

Skinner only cares about making money so he wants to put *Gusteau's* name on a tacky range of fast food. The great Auguste Gusteau would be horrified!

Aggressive stance

Sneaky

Until Linguini arrives, Chef Skinner stands to inherit the restaurant. He is determined that Linguini will not find out that he is really Gusteau's son.

Low-down chef

Scheming Skinner smells a rat. He knows that Linguini is hiding one somewhere, but he can't prove it. When he finally works out that the rat is the chef, Skinner kidnaps Remy and tries to make him create a range of frozen fast food for him.

Short legs

Did You Know?

Vertically challenged Chef Skinner is obsessed with looking taller. He wears an extra large chef's hat, but still needs a ladder to taste the soup!

COLETTE

AS THE ONLY female chef working at *Gusteau's*, Colette has had to be tough to survive. She is often the first person to arrive in the morning and the last one to leave at night. She is determined to be a top chef. But underneath her hard-baked exterior, Colette is sweet and kind.

Did You Know?
Colette's preferred mode of transport is a powerful motorbike. She loves to ride around Paris on it.

Getting fresh
Colette can tell if a loaf of bread is fresh just by tapping it. To her, a fresh loaf sounds like sweet music!

Spotless white uniform

Busy hands

Follow the recipe!
Colette always follows Gusteau's original recipes to the letter. She truly believes in his motto that anyone can cook—even the garbage boy. Or a rat!

"You are one of us now."

Tough teacher
Colette is assigned to teach rookie chef Linguini the basics. At first, she is very strict, but as Linguini proves to be a willing and grateful pupil, Colette starts to like him. And when he kisses her (thanks to Remy, of course) she starts to do more than just like him...

Standing up for others
Colette has strong principles and stands up for what, and whom, she believes in.

Sensible, non-slip shoes

EMILE

RATATOUILLE

REMY'S BIG BROTHER is a picky eater—whatever he picks up, he eats. Emile is happy to eat garbage and doesn't understand Remy's love of fine food or his habit of washing his paws before eating. However, easy-going Emile accepts that his brother is different and goes along with all his ideas, no matter how weird or dangerous they are!

Did You Know?
Emile has two great fears in life—being hungry, and being struck by lightning!

Caught!
For once, Emile is not thinking about food. Thanks to his little brother, he is in danger of being shot by a little old lady!

"You have a gift!"

Greedy rat
Remy's new job is a dream come true for Emile and he goes crazy in the larder.

Teamwork
The two brothers have very different goals in life—Remy wants to cook food and Emile just wants to eat it—but they are the best of friends.

Cheerful smile

A handy snack

Big brother
Emile loves food, but he loves his brother more. He is the only one who knows about Remy's interest in the world of humans and his dream to become a chef. The two brothers share all their secrets—well, they would if Emile had any!

Full belly

DJANGO

REMY'S DAD HAS no problem with the way rats live or what they eat. To Django, taking food isn't stealing, if nobody wants it. As the rat colony's leader, it is his job to keep the pack together and safe from the rats' greatest enemy—humans. If only he could make his youngest son understand that he is just trying to protect him.

Food advice
Django thinks that being fussy about food is a recipe for disaster. He worries that a sensitive rat like Remy won't survive in the real world. Food is fuel, nothing more.

Protective Dad
Django loves both his sons, but Remy is definitely more high-maintenance. Django worries that his youngest son is putting himself and their colony in danger by getting caught up in the world of humans. After all, what's so wrong with being a rat?

Shaggy gray fur

Extra-long nose

"Shut up and eat your garbage!"

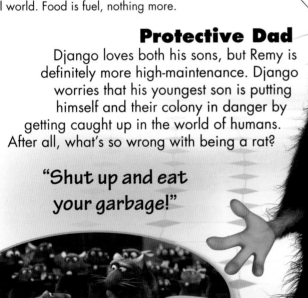

Family man
Django doesn't agree with Remy's career choices, but when his son needs help, he is there for him. If Remy needs some kitchen staff, then Django and his colony will scrub up and pitch in!

167

GUSTEAU

RATATOUILLE

ONCE CONSIDERED the finest chef in Paris, Auguste Gusteau ran a five-star restaurant, wrote a world-famous cookbook, and also starred in his own TV cooking show. Unfortunately, a bad review of his restaurant by food critic Anton Ego cost Gusteau one of his stars and broke the now four-star chef's heart.

Bright lights
Before Ego's review, *Gusteau's* was the most fashionable restaurant in Paris and was fully booked five months in advance.

Anyone can cook

Auguste Gusteau was the youngest chef ever to get a five-star rating. But despite being a culinary genius, he believed that creativity could come from anyone, anywhere. His cookbook, *Anyone Can Cook* is budding chef Remy's most cherished possession.

Extra-slim chef's hat

"Anyone can cook, but only the fearless can be great."

Did You Know?
When Gusteau died, his restaurant lost another of its stars. The now three-star restaurant is a shadow of its former glories.

Ghostly white chef uniform

Friend in need

Alone in Paris, Remy could really use a friend. Somehow, the spirit of Chef Gusteau appears to guide him. Is he real? Remy doesn't know, but, real or not, he helps the talented rat believe in himself.

ANTON EGO

THE WORLD'S most feared food critic loves to dish out cutting criticisms. Ego's reviews can make or break a chef's reputation, but the fussy foodie is extremely hard to please and few restaurants ever meet his high standards. He is an expert on fine food, but doesn't seem to find much pleasure in eating it.

Long, bony fingers

Did You Know?
Ego has a loyal butler named Ambritser. The poor man is terrified of his brooding boss.

Food snob
Ego's beliefs are the complete opposite to Gusteau's. The culinary connoisseur does not believe that just anyone can cook. Certainly not a rat!

Hard to please
Remy and Linguini are creating a sensation in *Gusteau's* kitchen, but their success brings an unwelcome visitor—Anton Ego. The cranky critic demands to be hit with Linguini's "best shot." He doesn't expect to be impressed.

Happy memories
One bite of Remy's ratatouille and Anton Ego's cold heart melts. His big ego disappears as he remembers a little Ego whose mother comforted him with simple food, seasoned with love.

Long, skinny legs

"I take cooking very seriously."

A new Anton
Eating Remy's food changes Anton Ego forever. He becomes a happier person and learns to really love food again.

THE CHEFS

A GOOD KITCHEN requires organization, teamwork, and a certain *je ne sais quoi*— and *Gusteau's* is no exception. Although Skinner is the boss, it is his highly trained, highly skilled, and highly unusual chefs who do all the really hard work.

Lalo—Fish Chef

Pompidou—Pastry Chef

Many hands
There's always something to do in the kitchen; peeling, chopping, slicing, dicing, roasting, toasting. And the hard work isn't over when the food is cooked. Then, the dirty dishes have to be washed!

The food chain
Every chef in the kitchen has a different specialty and they all work together to create gourmet meals to order. The chefs have to be talented and tough to survive in *Gusteau's* kitchen.

Horst—Assistant Head Chef

Larousse—Salad and Appetizer Chef

MUSTAFA

AS HEAD WAITER at *Gusteau's*, Mustafa is one of the most important people working in the restaurant. The chefs might think that the hard work happens in the kitchen, but it is Mustafa and his team of waiters who must ensure that customers have a first-rate dining experience.

Did You Know?
When Linguini and Remy's secret is revealed, Mustafa and the other waiters walk out. So Linguini pulls on his skates and waits on the whole restaurant by himself!

New creations
Linguini and Remy's success in the kitchen means that customers are demanding new, exciting dishes. And it's up to Mustafa to tell the chefs!

Rat!
When Mustafa grabs a dish from a passing trolley, he gets a little more than he expected. Fortunately Remy is too quick for him.

Tired eyes

Flushed cheeks

"Do you know what you'd like this evening, sir?"

Middle man
Plump Mustafa might look like he knows a lot about food, but he just serves it. If things go wrong in the kitchen, it is poor Mustafa who must explain things to the hungry customers. Being a head waiter is a very stressful job!

MABEL

WHAT A SWEET little old lady! She wouldn't hurt a fly (or rat), would she? Don't be fooled—this old-timer is armed and dangerous. Although she spends most of her time napping in front of the television, Mabel can leap into action when required. Like when she finds a colony of rats in her house…

Armed and dangerous
When Mabel realizes that her cozy cottage is home to a whole colony of rats, she only has one thought in her mind. Kill! Fortunately for them, the only thing she destroys is her own home.

Thick glasses

Floral hairnet

Cozy armchair

Missed!
Mabel follows the rats as they flee, but luckily she is an extremely bad shot!

Let sleeping ladies lie
Remy is spotted by the old lady while he is watching her television. When Mabel sees the rat, she doesn't hesitate: She grabs her shot gun from the umbrella stand and starts shooting.

NADAR LESSARD

SNEAKY SKINNER can't stand the thought that Linguini is Gusteau's rightful heir, so he makes a call to the Health Inspector to report a rat infestation. When Inspector Lessard arrives to investigate, he expects to find a rat or two. What he doesn't expect is a whole colony of rats, apparently running the kitchen and cooking the food!

Infestation
Poor Mr. Lessard has never seen so many rats in one kitchen!

Shocked expression

Official papers

Bad day
When the rats see the Health Inspector, they are smart enough to realize he means trouble. They work together to rope and tie him, then toss him in the cooler while they get on with cooking. At least it gives him time to chill out...

What a rat!
The rats have to release the Health Inspector eventually and he has no hesitation in shutting *Gusteau's* down. For good! Not to be beaten, Remy and Linguini open a new rat-friendly restaurant—
Le Ratatouille.

WALL•E

WALL•E

IT'S 2805 AND humans have left Earth covered in trash to live in luxury spaceships. Alone in a world covered in garbage, rusty but reliable WALL•E is the last clean-up unit on Earth. His job is to collect and cube garbage, but he brightens up his days by discovering treasures amongst the debris and listening to his favorite tune.

Trash to treasure
WALL•E loves to collect artifacts the human race left behind—even if he has no idea what they were actually used for.

Fantastic find
When WALL•E finds a living plant, he has no real idea of what it is. However, he senses that it is precious and is determined to look after it.

Did You Know?
When Wall•E shuts down, he pulls in all his limbs and goes into cube mode. This is also useful when he is scared!

Eyes work like binoculars

Extendable neck

Game change
The arrival of probe-bot EVE opens WALL•E up to a whole new world. When he shows his new friend the tiny green plant he has found, it triggers events that alter not only WALL•E's destiny, but also that of the entire human race.

Narrow escape
When WALL•E is helping EVE, he is blind to personal peril. He narrowly escapes being destroyed in the exploding escape pod—but saves the vital plant.

Hands to lift and sort trash

Treads help WALL•E move around on trash-covered terrain

EVE

COOL, SMART, and state of-the-art, this probe-bot is totally focused on her directive to discover plant life on Earth—until she meets WALL•E. It's not love at first sight for EVE, but the rusty robot soon brings fun, affection, and even a little dancing into her super-efficient world.

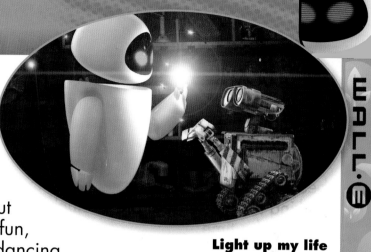

Light up my life

WALL•E shows how much he cares for EVE by sharing with her the most magical thing in his whole collection.

Shutdown

As soon as EVE sees WALL•E's plant, she shuts down. WALL•E fears that he has lost his new friend forever.

Eyes convey a variety of expressions

Dream team

Returning to space, EVE seems to forget her new friend, until she realizes that she needs him. EVE and WALL•E team up against bad bots Auto and GO-4 to save the planet and finally allow humans to go home to Earth.

Sleek body

Daring duo

Two bots are better than one when it comes to outwitting the security forces on board the *Axiom*. EVE provides flight power and WALL•E has a never-give-up attitude.

Arms function like wings

AUTO

THE *AXIOM'S* autopilot is programmed to handle the running of the ship, leaving very little for the human captain to do. The automated steering wheel has a beady red eye which sees everything, making his master feel pretty much useless most of the time.

Who's the boss?
The Captain thinks he calls the shots on the *Axiom*—but when it comes to the crunch, Auto is ready to confine his "master" to his quarters.

Secret orders
This sneaky robot has a secret: in the case of life ever being found on Earth, it must follow directive "A113," and prevent humans from returning home. The autopilot is programmed to do anything—even disobey the Captain—to carry out his orders.

No way home
Auto is convinced there is no possibility of returning to Earth—but the secret information he relies on is over seven hundred years out of date.

All-seeing eye

Did You Know?
Auto isn't really a bad guy—he's programmed to follow orders and there's nothing he can do about it!

Manual override
The mutinous machine has one weakness, and the Captain finally finds it. By switching control to manual, he puts mankind back in charge of its own destiny.

"Give me the plant."

Steering wheel

GO-4

THE HEAD OF security on the *Axiom*, this ruthless little machine knows everything that goes on aboard ship. He gives the steward-bots their orders and acts swiftly to send any renegade robots to the Repair Ward. GO-4 takes his responsibilities seriously and enjoys any opportunity to fire his red ray at trouble-makers.

Did You Know?

GO-4 ends up taking a trip out of the window of the Control Deck and lands in a heap on the Lido deck!

Self destruct

Faced with orders to destroy the plant immediately, GO-4 sneaks it into an escape pod, and sets it to self destruct. Luckily WALL•E is watching!

Glowing head

Ray power

He may only be a little guy, but GO-4 can make a big impact with his red ray. It creates a force-field that can even hold back an angry EVE.

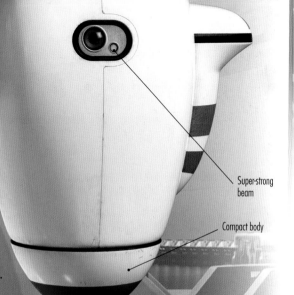

Super-strong beam

Compact body

Plant pilferer

GO-4 is not a bad bot, but he has been programmed by the Buy-n-Large Corporation to destroy any vegetation arriving from Earth. He intercepts the plant as soon as EVE arrives, and only WALL•E's heroics prevent GO-4 from destroying it.

M-O

KEEPING THE SHIP clean is all M-O cares about. He is the best in the business, able to spot contamination that humans can't even see. A rotating device attached to his arms can clean away all known dirt in a matter of seconds. Life for M-O is neat and tidy—until he meets WALL•E.

"Foreign contaminant!"

On the track
Diligent M-O is determined to track WALL•E's trail of contamination to its source and clean up the mess once and for all. Somewhere along the way his disgust turns to respect for a robot that can survive with all that filth.

Good clean fun
Even when the pair have become friends, the dedicated M-O can't resist giving his pal a little polish.

Friend or foe
The new arrival from Earth creates filth readings that go right off the chart. Well, he has spent his whole life working with trash. M-O is so intrigued by WALL•E's dirtiness that he follows the intruder around, and even ends up saving his life.

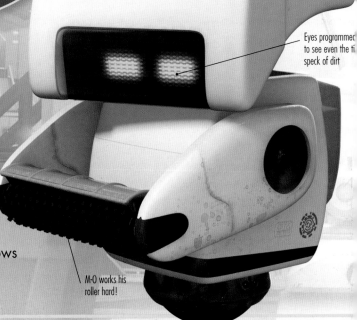

Eyes programmed to see even the tiniest speck of dirt

M-O works his roller hard!

BURN·E

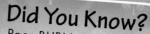

IT WOULD BE hard to find a more motivated worker on the *Axiom* than this Basic Utility Repair Nano Engineer, or BURN·E. The little repair-bot runs on a single track outside the ship and has a single-minded attitude towards getting the job done. Whether it's a humdrum light fixing, or major outside repairs, BURN·E takes it all in his stride.

Did You Know?
Poor BURN·E once got stuck to the outside of the ship during a hyperspace jump.

Protective eye shield

Hot stuff
BURN·E is an expert welder and repairing this exterior lamp on the *Axiom* really ought to be a trouble-free job. Unless WALL·E happens to be in the area…

Welder

Light to show the way

Locked out
Not every repair job goes completely to plan, however, and sometimes BURN·E can be a little accident prone. He can be unlucky, too, such as when he is locked outside the ship by WALL·E and EVE after their space flight. Luckily, BURN·E has just the tools to cut his way back in.

Track runner

WALL·E

THE CAPTAIN

BEING IN CHARGE of an executive starliner may sound like a stressful job, but life is easy for Captain B. McCrea. The ship is run by robots, so all he has to do is greet the passengers every morning and remind them what day it is. He gives a daily weather report: It's always a pleasant 72 degrees!

Groomed to go
The Captain is so reliant on machine pampering, he simply cannot face the day without his massage from a HAN-S bot and grooming by a PR-T bot.

Captain's hat

"I don't want to survive. I want to live."

Plump face

I'm in charge!
The captain proves that he is the man in charge when evidence arrives that the Earth is habitable again. He defies the orders of the BnL corporation (and his own autopilot) to launch a daring bid to take the human race home. But first, he'll have to practice using his legs again…

Did You Know?
In 2805, humans have grown so pampered and lazy that they move around on hover chairs and interact with each other using holo-screens.

Epaulet denotes rank

Precious plant

JOHN AND MARY

PAMPERED PASSENGERS on the *Axiom*, John and Mary have drifted out of the habit of doing things for themselves, just like the rest of mankind. However, chance encounters with WALL•E wake them both up out of their stupor. When the pair meet up they begin to enjoy life again.

WALL•E *(side tab)*

Down to earth
When the *Axiom* finally returns to Earth, John and Mary are there to witness the beginning of a new life. They share the moment when the Captain plants the first green shoot.

Meet WALL•E
John thinks WALL•E must be a drinks-bot when he first bumps into him. In fact, he tumbles right out of his chair trying to hand over his empty cup.

Did You Know?
Passengers like John and Mary have no need to buy new clothes. They just touch a screen and their day-suits change color instantly.

Typical human outfit

Surprised expression

New outlook
When John bumps into Mary, the two make an instant connection. They become so re-energized that when Auto tries to take control of the *Axiom*, John and Mary join forces to save the humans on board.

WALL·E

THE 5,000 passengers on board the *Axiom* are served by 500,000 robots. Whether they need a massage, a haircut, or even a game of golf, there is a bot, or several, who will do it for them. Thanks to the bots, humans don't have to do a thing for themselves.

GOLF-BOT
This hole-in-one expert even has his own caddy-bot to hold his clubs.

HAN-S
This massage-bot offers a stimulating facial or a soothing back-rub.

L-T
A mobile lamp will follow passengers anywhere they need to go.

VQ-M
Part of the cleaning team, the vacuum-bot scans the *Axiom* for minute dust particles.

PR-T
This beautician-bot is armed with lipstick, scissors, powder-puffs, tweezers, and much more.

BUF-R
Buffer-bots polish the *Axiom* paintwork to a shiny sheen.

DRINK-BOT
These eager servants are programmed to detect signs of thirst.

REPAIR-BOT
Repair-bots can be found all over the ship, quietly keeping things working.

SPRAY-BOT
Each spray-bot is equipped with anti-bacterial spray to keep the *Axiom* squeaky clean.

NAN-E
These bots deliver lessons in math and literacy. They can also change diapers in a crisis.

FOOD DISPENSER-BOT
Delivering meals straight to passengers' hover-chairs, these waiters can also display a picture menu on their screens.

TENNIS-BOT
The tennis-bot doesn't need a partner—it will happily play itself.

REJECT-BOTS

DOWN IN the Repair Ward, there is a bunch of machines the passengers are not supposed to see: the vacuum cleaner that sneezes, the light-bot that flickers, and the paint-bot that thinks it's Picasso. But no need to worry. All of these faulty machines are receiving some love, care, and a timely upgrade.

Danger ward
Rejects are kept in separate cubicles and held back by force-fields until they are safe to be let back into service. They are all fitted with a red diagnosis tool that monitors their condition and marks them out as possible rogue devices.

Reject HAN-S

Reject D-FIB

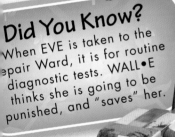

Did You Know?
When EVE is taken to the Repair Ward, it is for routine diagnostic tests. WALL·E thinks she is going to be punished, and "saves" her.

Reject BRL-A

Reject L-T

Reject paint-bot

Reject VQ-M

Rogue heroes
When WALL·E accidentally shuts down the power field holding the reject-bots, they make a bid for freedom, and hail WALL·E as their leader. The massage-bot proves handy in a battle, PR-T uses her vanity mirror to reflect laser beams, and BRL-A makes a great shield!

STEWARD-BOTS

CREATED TO maintain order on the ship, steward-bots have no ideas or personality of their own. They report to GO-4 and patrol the decks of the ship looking for signs of trouble. They pursue WALL•E and EVE in a desperate attempt to destroy the plant found on Earth.

"Halt!"

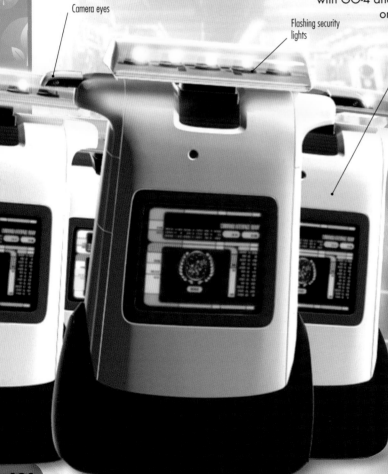

Camera eyes

Flashing security lights

Display panel

Welcome aboard

Nothing gets on board the *Axiom* without first being inspected by these snoopy stewards. Working closely with GO-4 and BUF-R, they make sure no contaminants or security risks of any kind sneak aboard.

Did You Know?

Stewards are linked to the communications web of the whole ship, and only have to see a rogue robot to transmit its image across every data system of the *Axiom*.

Freeze!

The stewards are armed with a freeze ray that can stop renegades in their tracks—if they can target them properly. Their front display panel can show a "stop" sign, an "on duty" screen, or a mugshot of the latest rogue robots they are hunting.

COCKROACH

THIS TOUGH LITTLE insect is a natural survivor, just like his friend WALL•E. They have been companions a long time and just seem to know how to get along. It's lucky the cockroach has a tough shell, as WALL•E often runs over it with his heavy treads.

Bug buddy
The cockroach is special to WALL•E, as it seems to be the only thing that shares an otherwise lifeless world with him. The robot always takes time out of his chores to check up on his tiny pal.

Patient pal
WALL•E knows his trip into space is going to be dangerous, so he makes sure his insect friend stays behind. On the robot's return, the cockroach is right where WALL•E left him.

Did You Know?
Cockroaches have amazing powers of survival. Many experts believe that they will remain on Earth if humans become extinct!

Long feelers

Loyal roach
This friendly bug helps bring WALL•E and EVE together when the robots are too shy to make the first move. The cockroach is a loyal creature and can be relied upon to stay home and stay safe while WALL•E heads off on his incredible adventure.

WALL • E's comeback
When EVE returns a damaged WALL•E to Earth, the cockroach shares her concern for his old friend. While EVE struggles to fix WALL•E, the loyal insect anxiously watches every step of the process.

Extra-tough wings

CARL FREDRICKSEN

IT'S HARD to imagine that grouchy Carl Fredricksen was once a small boy with dreams of becoming an explorer. But when a construction company tries to force him out of his house and into a retirement home, Carl hatches an exciting plan. He is off on an adventure—to South America's Paradise Falls!

"Cross my heart"
Carl's first encounter with future wife Ellie ended with a broken arm, and a promise that he'd take her to Paradise Falls one day. With Ellie gone, Carl decides to take their house instead!

"Oh, Ellie, what have I gotten myself into?"

Grape soda badge

Old-fashioned glasses

Hearing aid

Explorer Carl
Carl may be slower than he used to be, but he's certainly no less determined. By hook or by crook he'll get himself—and his new friends—to safety.

Well-loved armchair

Ready to rebel
Faced with losing his house, Carl imagines what Ellie would do. She sure wouldn't sit in an armchair, doing nothing. Inspired, Carl takes control of his life. His house and memories mean far more to him than obeying the rules.

ELLIE FREDRICKSEN

AS A CHILD, Ellie was determined, talkative, and a total tomboy. It was love at first sight for shy Carl. When Ellie told him her plans for the future, he promised that one day, they would go to Paradise Falls. However, after they got married, life got in the way and the couple never realized their dream.

Cheerful smile

"Thanks for the adventure—now go have a new one."

Paintbrush

Sweet dreams
Young Ellie recorded all the things she wanted to do in her precious Adventure Book. She showed it to Carl, because he shared her love of adventure.

Paint-splattered shirt

A lifelong dream
Ellie and Carl both worked at the local zoo. They saved for their Paradise Falls trip in a special jar. But whenever they got near to their target, everyday emergencies, such as fixing the car or repairing the roof, wiped out their savings. When Carl was finally able to buy the plane tickets, it was too late. Ellie was dying.

Happy couple
Before she passed away, Ellie wanted Carl to know that their life together had been enough of an adventure.

Retro outfit

Did You Know?
When Ellie and Carl first met, she gave him a badge made out of a grape soda bottle cap, which he still wears.

RUSSELL

ENERGETIC AND chatty, Russell is a Junior Wilderness Explorer but he is desperate to become a Senior Wilderness Explorer. All that stands between him and his goal is the Assisting the Elderly badge. However, when he tries to assist the elderly Mr. Fredricksen, Russell gets a lot more than he bargained for!

Wilderness Explorer cap

Snipe-catching net

A badge too far
Tracking a pesky snipe bird for Mr. Fredricksen, Russell ends up under the house—and then up in the air. Carl is certainly surprised to hear Russell's knock on the door.

"The wilderness must be explored!"

Tribe 54 kerchief

Real adventurer
Like all Wilderness Explorers, Russell is a keen animal lover. He is determined to protect the bird he's named "Kevin," and also recognizes that Dug will be a loyal pet.

Russell's badge collection

Good friends
The best moments in life, Russell and Carl discover, don't have to be wild adventures. They can be as ordinary as sharing an ice cream and counting cars.

KEVIN

WHEN Russell names the giant, colorful bird, he has no idea that "Kevin" is, in fact, female. Kevin spends her time trying to find food for her hungry chicks, and trying to avoid capture by Charles F. Muntz's dogs. A chocoholic, Kevin also gobbles Carl's walking stick and one of his helium balloons!

Long neck

Motherly instinct
Kevin likes Russell instantly, and not just because his pockets are full of chocolate. Missing her chicks, she is glad to have someone to mother. She tosses Russell into the air and rocks him to and fro.

Brightly-colored plumage

Shoo!
Having finally tracked her down, Dug wants to take Kevin prisoner. The problem is, she's twice his size!

Permanently hungry belly

Kevin's chicks
Like their mom, the cheeky chicks will try to eat anything. They slobber all over Carl's stick, so he decides to leave it behind.

Large, clawed feet

Up for fun
Kevin is unlike any other bird. Despite her size, she loves playing hide-and-seek. She dodges behind rocks when she's trying to tag-along after Russell and Carl, and then cleverly hides from Muntz among the balloons on Carl's house.

Did You Know?
Kevin is 12 feet (3.66 meters) tall. She lives with her babies inside a maze of twisty rocks called a labyrinth.

DUG

IT'S NOT HARD to love Dug—he is loyal, energetic, and completely adorable. He looks like a regular pet but, like all of Charles F. Muntz's dogs, he wears a collar that translates his thoughts into speech. Dug may not be the brightest dog in Muntz's pack, but he is a terrific tracker.

Did You Know?
Mean Alpha makes Dug wear the Cone of Shame to punish him when he loses Kevin.

"I've just met you and I love you."

Peekaboo!
Dug is half Golden Retriever, half Husky. It takes him a while to work out what's going on, but he gets there in the end. One day, he will be top dog!

Sensitive nose

A dog's life
Position in the pack is everything. That's why Dug is so keen to make a success of tracking Kevin—and why he hates having to admit that he let her get away.

Chosen master
Even loyal Dug can see that Carl will be a kinder master than Charles F. Muntz. Puppy-dog eyes won't win round the old man, but bravery in times of danger will.

Ever-wagging tail

Special collar

Perfect pet
All Dug is interested in is being liked—and squirrels. When Russell and Carl first encounter him, they can't believe their ears—a talking dog! Russell begs Carl to keep Dug as their pet.

CHARLES F. MUNTZ

AS ONE OF the world's most famous explorers, Charles F. Muntz traveled the globe in his *Spirit of Adventure* airship discovering rare plants and animals. He was a hero to every young adventurer, including Carl and Ellie. However, one ill-fated trip to Paradise Falls costs Muntz his reputation.

Unshakeable fury
Ignoring his creaking limbs, Muntz battles with Carl in his trophy room. Then, determined not to let Carl get away, Muntz scales the exterior of the airship.

Cold eyes

"Gray leader? Take down the house."

Battered leather flight jacket

Phoney!
When Muntz showed off the skeleton of a giant bird, the scientific world rejected him as a fraud.

Aggressive pose

Walking stick, or weapon?

Bird-brained
Years of fruitless searching for the mysterious giant bird have left Muntz a bitter man. Utterly obsessed, he'll stop at nothing to find his prize. However, to his dismay, an old man and a small boy beat him to it!

Did You Know?
No one believed that Muntz had really seen a giant bird so his membership with the National Explorer's Society was withdrawn.

ALPHA

AS HIS NAME suggests, Alpha is the leader of Muntz's pack of dogs. Ferocious and fierce, Alpha is a Doberman who loves being in control. The problem comes when his collar malfunctions—the other dogs find it hard to respect Alpha when his voice is so high and squeaky!

"You two shall have much rewardings from Master for the toil factor you wage."

Confused canines
Alpha's fond of using long, complicated sentences. That's all very well, but it sometimes leaves the pack baffled.

Hyper-sensitive ears

Mean eyes

Super snarler
Even when his voice sounds silly, Alpha can still be frightening. He makes poor Dug cower when he tells him off for losing the bird.

Malfunctioning collar

Bird hunter
Alpha prides himself on his superb tracking skills, yet he has failed to hunt down one of those giant birds that his master, Muntz, is so desperate to find. With his pointy ears and sensitive nose, it can only be a matter of time—can't it?

BETA AND GAMMA

ALPHA'S TRUSTED lieutenants are Beta, a beefy Rottweiler, and Gamma, a strong and sturdy Bulldog. They are stronger than the other members of the pack, and also slightly more intelligent. But only slightly.

Knowing their place

Alpha doesn't like Beta and Gamma laughing at his malfunctioning voice—he worries they might challenge his position. Beta defuses the situation by turning the conversation back around to Dug.

Did You Know?

Beta thinks Russell is a "small mailman" because of his Wilderness Explorer uniform.

Scared expression

Gamma the pilot

Muntz has trained some of his dogs to fly specially designed planes. Gamma controls his plane by biting the bone-shaped joystick.

"Oh, man, Master will not be pleased."

Special collar

Top trackers

Beta and Gamma help Alpha to track down Kevin and her new human pals. Their powerful senses of smell even pick up the scent of the chocolate in Russell's pocket—and Carl's denture cream.

Large paws

KING FERGUS

BIG, BRAVE King Fergus is a loving husband and father, and a kind ruler. His strength and courage once united the clans and brought peace to the Highlands. Now trouble is brewing in Fergus's own castle, and that peace is under threat.

Bear escape
King Fergus lost a leg in a famous battle with the demon bear, Mor'du. He'd love a chance to pay the bear back— and turn the beast into a rug!

Flaming red, curly hair

"Princess or not, learning to fight is essential."

Warm fur cloak

Old warrior
Fun-loving Fergus has a great sense of humor and always lives in the moment. He likes hunting, brawling, and eating huge dinners. When he thinks a bear is attacking his family, the King shows his tough side.

DunBroch plaid kilt

Wooden leg

Did You Know?
Fergus is a pretty easy-going guy, except when it comes to bears. He is determined to find Mor'du and protect his family.

QUEEN ELINOR

GRACIOUS QUEEN Elinor rules the kingdom with calm diplomacy. She is the perfect complement to her husband and together the king and queen keep the kingdom peaceful. However, there is one person that Elinor cannot seem to get along with—her daughter.

"The clans must know that the DunBrochs honor our commitments."

Simple crown, inlaid with jade

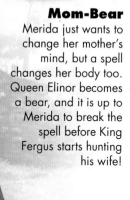

Traditional tapestry
Elinor stitched this tapestry. It symbolizes the love that binds her family together—until Merida rips it.

Regal pose

Tough lesson
Queen Elinor can't understand her daughter's point of view: Getting married is Merida's royal duty, so why won't she do it? However, spending some time as a bear helps Elinor to understand how Merida is feeling and the troubled mother and daughter finally reconnect.

Mom-Bear
Merida just wants to change her mother's mind, but a spell changes her body too. Queen Elinor becomes a bear, and it is up to Merida to break the spell before King Fergus starts hunting his wife!

Elegant green gown

PRINCESS MERIDA

FREE-SPIRITED MERIDA is certainly not her mother's idea of a perfect princess. Merida's favorite things are archery, sword fighting, and exploring the wild lands around her home, the Kingdom of DunBroch.

Daddy's girl
Merida has inherited her red hair and her love of adventure from her father, King Fergus. He gave Merida her first bow when she was a wee girl and loves to practice swordplay with her.

Trusty bow

Quiver of arrows

"I want my freedom."

Unruly red hair

Did You Know?
Merida is desperate to change her mother's mind—she will try anything, even a spell from a witch.

Steady steed
Merida's horse, Angus, has been her best friend since he was a foal. She can tell him anything and he loves to be part of her adventures.

Taking charge
Merida chooses an archery contest to decide her suitor, then wins it herself! Her Mom is angry because Merida's actions inadvertently threaten peace in the kingdom. It is up to Merida to make things right again.

Mom trouble
Lately, Merida and her Mom can't seem to get along. Queen Elinor thinks that Merida should get married, but Merida isn't ready for it.

THE TRIPLETS

MERIDA MIGHT NOT be the ideal princess, but her three younger brothers are trouble. Tripled! Princes Harris, Hamish, and Hubert are lovable little scamps who spend their time inventing new pranks to play on the unsuspecting inhabitants of the castle.

Big sis
The DunBroch children all have the same red curls and sense of fun. Harris, Hamish, and Hubert love to tease their big sister, but help her out when it counts.

Did You Know?
Each triplet always knows what the others are thinking, without words. They don't really need to speak to other people.

Three little bears
Getting into trouble is hungry work and the triplets are always looking for snacks. When they see the remains of a magical cake, they gobble it right up.

Mischievous expression

Familiar red hair

Family plaid

Royal trio
Being turned into bears doesn't bother the mischievous triplets one little bit. In fact, they quite like it! The three royal bears help their sister save their Mom, and play a few new tricks as well...

MOR'DU

THE LEGEND of the demon bear strikes fear into the hearts of all the clans. The enormous, vengeful Mor'du is said to roam the Highlands striking out at anyone who gets in his way. Unfortunately, this time it is Merida and her mother who cross his path.

Danger!
When King Fergus fought Mor'du, he was lucky to get away with at least three of his limbs intact. This time, Merida might not be so lucky...

Did You Know?

Mor'du attacked Fergus, Elinor, and Merida at a family picnic. It was before the triplets were even born.

Terrifying teeth

Evil eyes

Bad wish

Mor'du was once a prince who asked the Witch for a spell to grant him the strength of ten men. The prince got his wish, but it wasn't exactly what he wanted—the spell turned him into a bear.

Bear to bear
Elinor-Bear has the strength to finally defeat the demon bear. No one hurts her family!

THE WITCH

WHO ARE YOU calling a witch? This mysterious old lady prefers to be called a wood-carver. It's true that she does have a lot of wood carvings in her home, especially of bears. However, for a wood-carver, she seems to know an awful lot about making spells...

Home sweet home
The Witch lives in a tiny run-down old cottage, deep in an overgrown wood. It is very difficult to find without help.

Wise old lady
The only way to get to the Witch's cottage is with the help of mysterious forest spirits called will o' the wisps. It means that the old lady doesn't get a lot of company, but those who do seek her out always seem to need her help with something big.

Talkative black crow

Spell cake
The Witch gives good advice, but it's a shame that no one ever takes it! Merida thinks that the Witch's cake will solve her problems with her mother, but she needs to listen to her words too.

Long, bony fingers

"Fate be changed, look inside, mend the bond, torn by pride."

Shabby green cape

LORD MACGUFFIN

CLAN MACGUFFIN lives in the rainy coastal area of Scotland and speaks in a strongly accented dialect that is very hard for other folk to understand. Lord MacGuffin is the leader of this clan, and is as strong as a Highland bull. He has a deep booming voice that can be heard for miles around.

Did You Know?
The only thing louder than Lord MacGuffin's speaking voice is his laugh, which has been known to shake the kingdom.

"Let these lads try and win her heart before they win her hand...if they can!"

Full beard

Stylish braids

My boy
Lord MacGuffin is proud of his strapping son and hopes that he will one day become a strong leader, just like him.

Debt of honor
King Fergus once saved MacGuffin from a deadly arrow. MacGuffin repaid the favor by helping Fergus in his first battle with Mor'du. Now, MacGuffin has his heart set on his son marrying Fergus's daughter.

MacGuffin clan tartan

Strong arms

YOUNG MACGUFFIN

ACCORDING TO HIS proud Dad, Young MacGuffin once vanquished 2,000 foes with his bare hands. That might not be strictly true, but the young lord is certainly capable of handling himself in a brawl, hunting a wild bear or two, or tossing a caber in some Highland games.

"After we slaughter the beast, we'll be heroes!"

Big, strong neck

Slight beard

Not his sport
Young MacGuffin excels at tough guy sports, but he is way off the mark when it comes to archery.

Brawny boy
He might be brave on the battlefield, but when it comes to speaking in public, Young MacGuffin is completely tongue-tied. However, it doesn't really matter what the shy young man says, as no one can actually understand his accent!

Did You Know?
Young MacGuffin tries to impress Merida by snapping logs, but she finds it funny, not romantic!

Sporran

Surprisingly small feet

LORD DINGWALL

CLAN DINGWALL's men are not renowned for their height or brawn. However, whatever they lack in stature, they make up for in spirit. Lord Dingwall is the oldest of the four clan leaders, but he likes a brawl just as much as the rest of them!

Wild hair

Proud dad
As Lord Dingwall boasts about his son, the rest of the clans look impressed, until the real Wee Dingwall steps out from behind the muscly warrior.

"Now what about this suitor business?"

True Scot
Lord Dingwall is a traditional Scotsman when it comes to what he wears beneath his kilt. And he doesn't care who knows it!

Proud Dad
Lord Dingwall is proud of his son, and likes to boast about all of his achievements. Although Wee Dingwall doesn't quite live up to expectations, his Dad is still keen for him to marry Princess Merida.

Dingwall clan plaid

WEE DINGWALL

FATHER AND SON Dingwall share the same wild, wiry hair and small stature, but Wee Dingwall isn't quite as fiery-tempered as his father. He is also not as keen on the idea of marriage to Princess Merida as Lord Dingwall is, but he obediently enters the archery contest and tries his best to win.

Long neck

Strong teeth

Biting back

Wee Dingwall might not be as big as Young MacGufffin or as tough as Young Macintosh, but he can still look after himself in a battle. His secret weapon? He bites!

Secret talent

Wee Dingwall isn't tall, or strong, or clever, but he has other skills. When given a bow, he would rather pluck it like a harp than shoot an arrow. Maybe his music could win Merida's heart? Maybe not...

Second place

Wee Dingwall proves to be a better archer than his fellow suitors. However, none of them are a match for Merida.

Oversized sporran

Skinny legs

"I dinnae pick her out. It was your idea."

Did You Know?

Dingwall clan colors represent the thistle and heather from the Highland countryside.

LORD MACINTOSH

CLAN MACINTOSH come from the remote Isle of Skye. Wiry warrior Lord Macintosh is so tough that he doesn't even wear an undershirt! The proud Dad boasts about the time that his brave son defended their lands from Northern foes.

Boastful Dad
Lord Macintosh loves to tell tall tales about his son's achievements, including the time he vanquished 1,000 foes with his sword!

Skinny body

"Och, we've all heard that tale!"

Blue war paint

Rivals
The three lords all want their sons to win Princess Merida's hand, but Merida doesn't want any of them!

Macintosh family plaid

Touchy guy
Lord Macintosh likes to look the part of the tough warrior, but, as with his son, his appearance is deceptive. The lanky Lord is extremely suspicious and always thinks that he is being treated unfairly.

Weapon of choice
Lord Macintosh's favorite weapon is a type of club—known as a mace. It is great for hitting enemies, hard.

Mace

HE CERTAINLY LOOKS like a handsome warrior, with his flowing locks and fierce expression. However, Young Macintosh is a very poor loser. If things don't go his way, the not-so-tough young lord is likely to throw a tantrum or burst into tears. That's definitely not the way to Merida's heart.

Proud expression

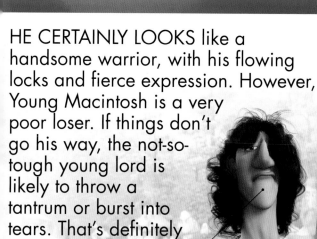

Big kid
Young Macintosh's failure to impress in the archery contest hits him hard. He bawls like a spoilt baby, in front of everyone!

Large sword

Big head
Young Macintosh loves to show off and is used to being cheered by crowds of adoring ladies. However, when Merida chooses an archery contest to decide her suitor, the would-be warrior soon shows his true colors.

Pick me!
Big-headed Young Macintosh is confident that Princess Merida will pick him because he is stronger, braver, and more handsome than her other suitors.

"Give us our say in choosin' our own fate!"

Did You Know?
Young Macintosh and his father like to decorate their bodies with blue paint to intimidate their enemies.

INDEX

DK

LONDON, NEW YORK, MELBOURNE,
MUNICH, AND DELHI

Editor Jo Casey
Design Assistant Satvir Sihota
Designers Richard Horsford, Poppy Joslin, Rhys Thomas
Design Manager Ron Stobbart
Publishing Manager Catherine Saunders
Art Director Lisa Lanzarini
Publisher Simon Beecroft
Publishing Director Alex Allan
Pre-Producer Siu Yin Chan
Senior Producer Shabana Shakir

First published in the United States in 2012
by DK Publishing
375 Hudson Street, New York, New York 10014

10 9 8 7 6 5 4 3 2 1
001-182934-Oct/12

Color reproduction by MDP, UK
Printed and bound at Leo Paper Products Ltd, China

Acknowledgments
The publisher would like to thank Pamela Afram, Emma Grange, Julia
March, and Victoria Taylor at DK for editorial assistance, Lynne Moulding at DK
for design assistance, and Chelsea Alon, Chuck Wilson, Scott Tilley, Tony Fejeran,
Deborah Boone, and LeighAnna MacFadden at Disney Publishing

Discover more at
www.dk.com